Cinema Contra Cinema
The Collected Essays of Jack Sargeant
© 1998 Jack Sargeant

First published 1999 by:
Fringecore
P.O.Box 165
2600 Berchem 1
Belgium
info@fringecore.com
www.fringecore.com
© 1999 Fringecore

ISBN: 90-76207-50-X

All rights reserved. No part of this publication may be reproduced, transmitted or stored in a retrieval system, in any form or by any means, without permission in writing from the publishers.

Acknowledgements:

Typeset design and execution by Red Right Hand and Jack Sargeant.

Photographs reproduced by courtesy of copyright holders: Eric Brummer, Jeff Keen, Modi/Modivation, Tyler Hubby, Charles Pinion/Fireball, Tessa Hughes-Freeland & Ela Troyano, Beth B/B Movies, Marne Lucas, Huck Botko, Julie Peasley, Blunt Cut, Mark Hejnar, Peter Strickland/Peripheral, Monte Cazazza and Richard Kern.

Readers of this volume are assumed to be mature adults and neither the author, publishers or distributors are responsible for the use or misuse of the information contained within this volume.

Fringecore – The international forum for progressive culture.

Cinema Contra Cinema

For Stephanie Watson, Billy Chainsaw, Lydia Lunch, and Monte Cazazza, for their limitless support.

Contents

Introduction **8**

Chewing Bubblegum and Underground Cinema:
Peter Strickland – England's Finest Independent Filmmaker **13**

Aural Celluloid: Ten Brief Notes and Observations
on Underground Film and Underground Music **27**

Tracing the Edge of Power: A Brief Introduction to the Film and Art of Beth B **33**

Screening Transgressive Desires:
David Cronenberg's *Crash* and Bruce LaBruce's *Hustler White* **57**

Louder, Faster, Shorter: The Manny and Modi Shorts **61**

Human Wave: The Videos of Raymond Pettibon **69**

Plastic Porn Visionary: The Films of Eric Brummer **75**

Swallow: The Bad Taste of Sweet Vengeance of Huck Botko **89**

Pulp Videos: The Twisted World of Charles Pinion **95**

Documenting the Underground **125**

True Stories About True Gore: The World of Monte Cazazza **131**

Baby Blatzo Vs Dr. Gaz: The Cinematic Visions of Mr. Soft Eliminator Jeff Keen **137**

An Introduction to the Films of Tyler Hubby **155**

Dephtography and Non-Linear Animation: The World of M. Henry Jones **167**

No Beer, Some Movies, And a Lot of Rain:
The 4th Chicago Underground Film Festival Diary **177**

Appendix **189**

Bibliography **190**

An Introduction

Cinema Contra Cinema is a collection of texts, essays and interviews, which focus on the largely neglected terrain of underground film and video. These works represent a species which may be said to exist in a curious cultural economy to the recognizable forms of visual entertainment, maintaining an ambiguous and complex network of relationships to the dominant modes of cinema, from the antithetical to the symbiotic.

Whilst dominant cinema is characterized by tendencies towards narrative closure and textual and aesthetic verisimilitude, the works which are explored in this volume frequently challenge the acceptable and familiar notions dictated by the stifling, unifying tendencies of mainstream entertainment. Instead of presenting a seamless naturalism, the filmmakers whose work is explored deliberately explode homogenizing conventions via a multiplicity of techniques, ranging from the re-incorporation of existing footage into new critical structures as manifested in *True Gore*, to the celebration of cinema-as-entertainment as manifestation-of-pure-velocity-and-excess in the pedal-to-the-metal roar of Eric Brummer's excessive animated splatterfests: action movies *in extremis*.

Other filmmakers included in this volume question the very nature of the audience's relationship to the visual experience of film; M. Henry Jones' dephtographic work opens up the visual plane in dimensions previously unrecognized by the majority of filmmakers, while Tyler Hubby's work focuses on the very relationship between audience and temporality, celebrating commonplace events in actual time. What these filmmakers, whose work is explored in these texts, can be said to share is a desire to play unrestrained within the terrain of the visual, free from the political, social, cultural and financial constraints of dominant cinema.

Even the few mainstream independent films explored in this book are produced by celebrated 'auteurs' whose work delineates a space within feature film production that allows for the introduction of controversial thematics and ideas, predominantly the representation of what would commonly be viewed as manifestations of `perverse' sexuality.

Cinema Contra Cinema does not seek to explore or delineate any universal truths about underground film, nor does it offer a glimpse at any new trend – rather, these essays exist as individual lines of flight, moving simultaneously in multiple directions, and examining new potentialities for visual pleasures.

This collection was aided by the following individuals whose friendship and support remains invaluable: Beth B, Jay Bliznick, Blunt Cut, Brighton Cinematheque, Eric Brummer, Chris Campion, Stuart Caine, Andrew Clare, Cole, Fringecore, Bobby Gillespie, Michelle Handelman, Mark Hejnar, the Horse Hospital, Karen Howel, Tyler Hubby, Tessa Hughes-Freeland, Donna Jagela, M. Henry Jones, Jeff Keen, Richard Kern, Marne Lucas, Carlo McCormick, Modi, Jim Morton, My Eyes! My Eyes!, Charles Pinion, James Pyman, Mike Shreeve, Wendy Soloman, Peter, Cathi Unsworth, Bryan Wendorf, Rob Whalley, Caspar D. Williams, James Williamson, my family and, no doubt, several erroneous omissions.

A Note On The Text

This collection represents a sample of three years of writing on underground and independent cinema. When writing for a publication the style and length of a piece is dictated by spatial and editorial concerns, and thus, these essays and interviews were written to the (demands and) specifications of various editors. Often these pieces were written whilst travelling – frequently on borrowed computers, sometimes in notebooks, and occasionally on the backs of scraps of paper – they consequently represent a different approach to writing than my previous works. Whilst I have tried to keep the essays as they were originally published, in some cases they have been re-edited, and where necessary, annotated with more thorough footnotes and references. Where possible, however, they have been left unchanged.

Chewing Bubblegum and Underground Cinema

Peter Strickland – England's Finest Independent Filmmaker

Peter Strickland was twenty when he started shooting his 16mm film **Bubblegum** (1996), and twenty three when he finally finished it. That is a lot of hard work. The film stars Cinema Of Transgression maestro Nick Zedd, and one time Warhol associate and off-off-Broadway star, Holly Woodlawn. In **Bubblegum**, Holly plays a woman obsessed by a rockstar, and her fantasies about him sustain her in the face of the shear bludgeoning loneliness of her life, every time she sees a star she remembers "close your eyes and make a wish". Nick Zedd, meanwhile, is cast as a sleazeball who poses as the rock star – "it's all in the shoes" drawls Zedd in a fake Memphis accent. Naturally, when these two lonely souls meet, tragedy is inevitable, but Strickland handles the direction well, and the narrative never becomes weighed down by pathos, instead both Woodlawn and Zedd inject their tragic roles with enough nervous energy - and a little camp - to give the whole movie a feeling reminiscent of either Rainer Werner Fassbinder's **Angst essen Seele auf** (aka **Fear Eats The Soul**, 1974), or Mike and George Kuchar's 8mm underground melodramas. Since it was completed last August, **Bubblegum** has played at the Chicago Underground Film festival, the Berlin Film Festival, the Edinburgh Film Festival, and been picked up for a four-month stint on Air New Zealand; as Peter says "it's great that families going on holiday get to see two underground icons from successive generations together on screen, thousands of feet up in the sky."

Prior to making **Bubblegum,** Strickland directed a string of movies, on both Super 8 and video, most of which have never been released, including: **Rising Within The Realms Of Sleep** (1992/3), **Between God And Inspiration Lie Heaven And Hell** (1993), **Relapse** (1993/4), **Fall-out** (1993/4), and an optically distorted hermeneutic interpretation of a phlebotomical performance by Otter[1] entitled **Intravista** (1994/5). He has recently completed **Bubblegum (Special Edition)** (1997), a postmodern re-make, shot and edited in one day on video and scripted in Japanese. He is currently developing two new projects, a short film based around The Sonic Catering Band, who make culinary landscape music for the Netherlands based Staalplaat label, and a feature film in Greek, the details of which he won't divulge.

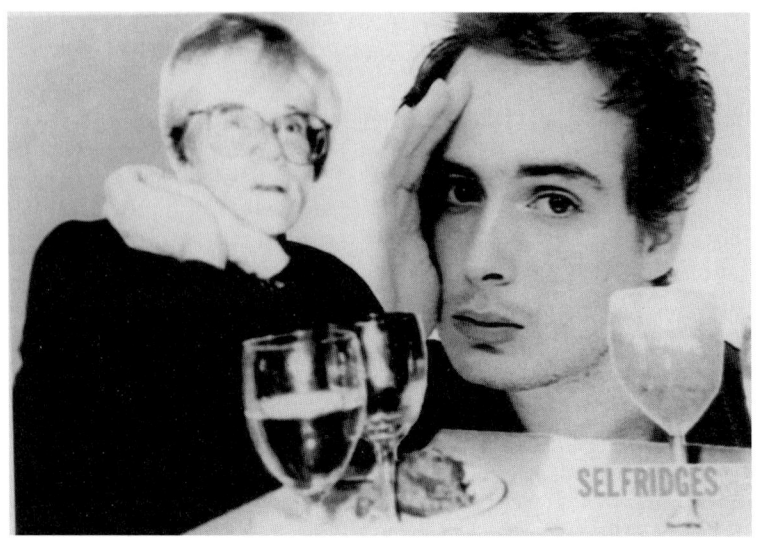
Andy Warhol/Peter Strickland (Photo Booth: Selfridges Warhol Party May 1998)

Peter was interviewed shortly before the English premier of **Bubblegum**, and then again shortly before the premier of the special edition of the film.

Jack Sargeant: I want to ask you first about your interest in the underground, what was your relationship to it, because **Bubblegum** *is such a - for want of a better word - "sweet" movie...?*

Peter Strickland: I was trying to counteract the whole underground thing - that whole thing about making films out of revenge – to piss people off. It's a lot better if you get revenge by seducing people and making them laugh. It's a much better way of pissing people off. I produced something that was in the tradition of underground and extreme – or extreme to that kind of audience –whereas like, I had reverse extremism, where it was so clean, and so tame. Purely for that reason it was unexpectedly different. Take people by surprise, really. That was the main reason behind it. I don't see myself doing another film like that.

JS: *How did you first learn about the underground, when did you first become aware of the possibilities of a cinema which could exist contra to the mainstream?*

PS: When I was 16 I went to the Scala[2], and saw **Eraserhead** (David Lynch, 1978) for the first time in February 1990. I had no real concept of that kind of cinema. I was basically just another kid from [the town of] Reading who wanted to make films, but felt frustrated with what was on offer. You can imagine what a real dive into the ocean it was from having seen the latest Tom Cruise flick back then at the local Odeon [a British multiplex chain], to **Eraserhead** at the Scala. It was so vivid, I can still recall the smell of the soap I washed my hands with. Ultimately the whole experience ended up binding me, because it was so liberating. I spent years suffering from an anxiety of influence, just trying to snap out of the spell that **Eraserhead** cast. It just turned me...

I was thinking seriously about making films around '89, about a year before. I always knew that there was an underground but I just didn't know how to get to it. You see something like **Eraserhead** and it fits in... that was really my film education, going to the Scala: Tarkovsky[3], Kaurismaki[4], Bunuel[5], anyone and everyone, you know, all the usual names, along with all the really unheard of stuff. I first heard of Kern[6], Zedd, and the whole Super 8 scum-bag scene around then, although for some reason I didn't go to the [Richard Kern] screening. Only I kept the flyer.

It was my big ambition to get a film shown there but obviously I didn't quite make it in time. Recently I met Jane Giles who used to program the Scala, she said they definitely would have shown **Bubblegum** if it was still open, so I guess that's some sort of recompense.

JS: *Then what happened – after becoming aware of the whole scene... the genealogy?*

PS: I tried to go to [film] school, but didn't get anywhere...

JS: That was probably for the best...

PS: Well, now it's like a blessing in disguise. I just kept going really. I dabbled in some theater stuff; I directed an adaptation of [Kafka's] *Metamorphosis* in 1992. And I was doing Super 8 stuff, on and off, ever since I saw **Eraserhead**. I finally started doing stuff that I could show people around 1992.

JS: When did you make that film of Otter? What was it called... didn't the name change?

PS: It's got different names all the time, it was called **Bloodshot**, then it was called **Intravista**. I shot it when I first went to New York, in 1994, at the Cooler, where Otter was doing her vampire act. It was all pretty frenzied so I only got a few seconds of usable footage. I had access to this computer where I could really do what I wanted for the first time, and just chose to make the kind of film I'd been trying to make for ages.

JS: It's a bit of an 'art film'...

PS: It's a bit of an art film. And I'm not sure about it now. What I was trying to do was, I'm kind of interested in juxtaposing different styles and opening... just trying to get a some kind of new language or something. I got heavily into [Stan] Brackhage[7] in that period. All that stuff, Michael Snow[8], things like that. But it gets weird.

I hadn't actually seen any of those films – I didn't know how to – I just read about them, and imagined how they'd be. And **Flaming Creatures**[9], I've read about since I was 18. I was just interested in these two, kind of, opposite undergrounds, which maybe weren't quite so opposite as it seems. Like this kind of very orgiastic subject matter, and then stuff like Michael Snow, who are very theoretical and scientific in their approach.

JS: And you were sort of mixing the two styles, with this image, but distorted and slowed down so much...

PS: Its like minimal maximal, repeats, like LaMonte Young[10]. Something in the spirit of the minimalist music of Steve Reich[11] or Philip Glass[12], where images would take on a notational value and just build from incredibly simple parts to something quite abstract and complex. ...So what you have is a set of three

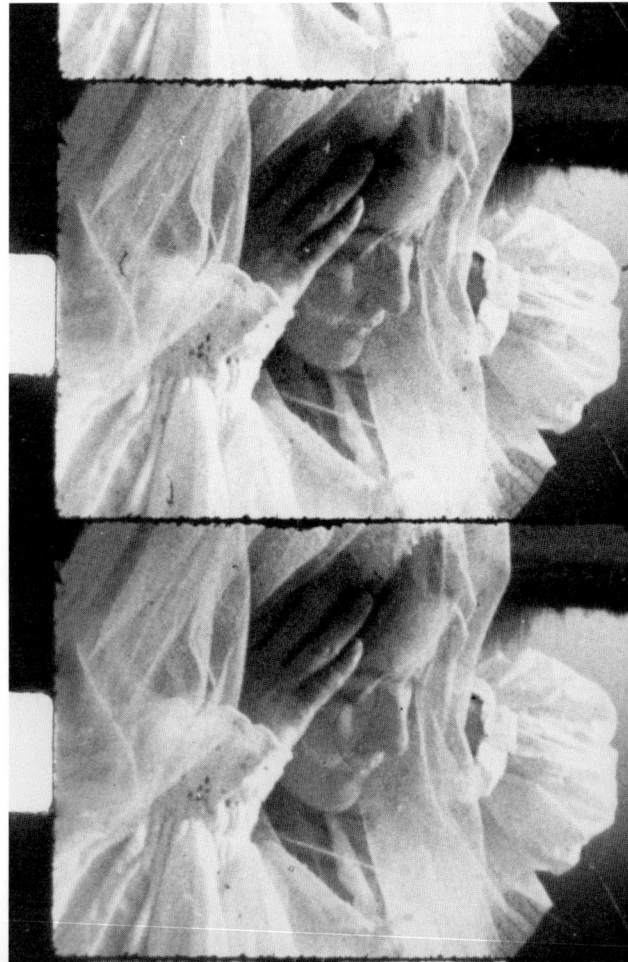

Georgina Arando in Super 8 blowup from *Rising Within the Realms of Sleep*
[Photo by Peter Strickland]

images that make up a movement running at 5% of the normal speed, repeated five times, then at 10% [of normal speed] repeated five times, then 15% five times, and so on till you get to 100% which is normal speed, then some new codas are introduced and the number of repeats and the jump in increases doubles until you get to 1000% and near white-out. By that time you have patterns within patterns within patterns, and it becomes like a moving lattice. Two groups, Main and Nurse With Wound were going to do the soundtracks, but I'm skeptical whether it's ever going to happen. As far as I am concerned, the film's finished and I really can't be asked to chase people up. Maybe one day I'll do something with all of this, only at the moment, apart from **Bubblegum**, all my films just sit around in my bedroom.

JS: Stylistically it is also similar to the work of Tony Conrad[13]..

PS: It's funny that you mention that. He was going to do a cut-up of the original film. But he didn't like it. (laughs) I spent a day with him, he is really

Holly Woodlawn / Peter Strickland Millenium Mens` / E 4th St., NYC Sept. 1995
[Photo by Tessa Hughes Freeland]

interesting. I met him two years ago. He was playing in London with Faust and I got the London Musicians' Collective to arrange a meeting. Nothing really came out of it apart from a pleasant stroll around London.

JS: So when did you start to shoot **Bubblegum**?

PS: I started in February 1994, it took a long time; two and a half years. I started the way everybody does... applied for sponsorship and grants. Didn't get anything. The same as everyone. Got a bit of local press...

JS: That can always help. I think John Waters was once photographed shooting a movie called **Dorothy, The Kansas City Pot Head**[14], and that made all the papers, but there was never any film in the camera. He just needed the publicity.

PS: That's what I was trying to do, but I didn't get anywhere really, it became

Toshihide Nukui & Kazuko Hohki in *Bubblegum* (Special Edition) aka *Special Bubblegum*
[Photo 1997 Peter Strickland]

Nick Zedd in *Bubblegum* at Max Fish, Ludlow St., NYC [Photo by Peter Strickland]

Nick Zedd/Holly Woodlawn on 5th Avenue / Sept. 1995 [Photo by Peter Strickland]

a laughing matter... here is this guy making a film who can't do it. This kept on dragging on.

JS: So how did you get Nick Zedd and Holly Woodlawn involved in the project?

PS: I got Holly involved in about May. I didn't even know she was alive. I rang loads of places...Warhol's film [distributors], the British Film Institute.... I still couldn't get hold of her (actually, when they wanted to get hold of her for a recent Warhol season they actually phoned me up). But, there was a documentary on her – not her but the Velvet Underground – on the BBC, so I rang up the BBC got hold of the guy who produced it, he gave me her agent's number. I sent the script.. she was incredibly easy going, she said "yeah" she'd do it.

I met Zedd through Richard Kern, who passed on his number, having been asked himself to play the role. My first choice for the part was Lux Interior, only I can't quite remember what happened with that. Nick was then next on the wish list, only I convinced myself it wouldn't work out. I had heard too many bad stories about him when I was in New York, and I could just imagine a response saying "I read your screenplay with interest, only I didn't happen to think it was particularly transgressive". It turned out, almost a year later, after no luck with Jon Spencer or Richard Kern, that he was interested, if only because of Holly Woodlawn's involvement.

JS: What was Nick like to work with?

PS: In terms of him cooperating, he was all in all, pretty much all right. I think, now and again, he had to remind himself that he was Nick Zedd, and forcefully impinge his own opinions on how things should go. When I first met him he gave me a revised copy of my script, and within hours threatened to walk out on the film if I didn't change certain words. I don't believe in being bloody minded and some of the changes made more sense, only a few of his suggestions were so out of sync with what I was getting at that we'd just find ourselves reaching a stalemate.

After several days I won him round to my way of thinking just for the sake of a few words here or there, only to me that is vital. In general, I think, unless otherwise intended, all art should involve no collaboration or compromises. You can lose your lead actor and director of photography, and you'll still pretty much get the same film with a

Bubblegum frame blow-up

replacement, only if you lose your director you're left with nothing but resources. Who - after all - wants films made by a committee? That's why there is so much crap out there, because people sit around tables too much, neutralizing each other's ideas. As long as a film has a singular vision behind it then it can't fail on a certain level, and Ed Wood[15] is a testament to that.

All my favorite films are by people who are wholly expunging themselves into their work. As long as someone is working their character into something and not premeditating what someone else might think then it doesn't ultimately matter whether it's good or bad. All that bullshit about prejudging your audience, making sure their attention is held. How can you possibly prejudge an audience? It's every filmmaker's right – no matter how good or bad – to have complete control. Obviously I want the film to go down well with an audience, but not at the expense of compromise.

But Nick Zedd, he really did turn out to be surprisingly supportive,

Box art from *Bubblegum* VHS cassette

Toshihide Nukui learning lines for *Bubblegum Special Edition* March '97 - Reading [Photo by Peter Strickland]

bar the occasional moment. All those tales about him, I don't know if they're true or not. I suppose if people still talk about you, you're doing okay.

JS: *When we've spoken in the past you've always drawn a distance on camp in your work, you don't seem to be a fan, but* **Bubblegum** *has some incredibly camp elements, care to comment?*

PS: This camp thing is a funny one. I can certainly appreciate the camp appeal in **Bubblegum**, but it wasn't the way I envisaged it. My thinking behind it was more on the lines of absurdism and artifice, which is where camp can all too easily arise from. I don't have a problem with the film being seen that way, only it's just not me. Ironically, I quite like camp cinema, but I'm not interested in making stuff like that. I usually hate exaggerated acting, which is a slight contradiction with what I've said... but with Nick, I think he got it just right for the part he was playing. He [is cast as] a fake who spends all his time hamming it up, so there you go.

JS: *All of your films have different stylistic approaches, why is that?*

PS: All my films are different in so far as I'm still finding my way around. In theory, I'm just kicking in the womb, as you are not officially a filmmaker until you've made your first feature. If you excluded **Bubblegum**, then you could easily trace a stylistic link through my stuff, quite easily. Only **Bubblegum** kind of messed all that up, which is never a bad thing. I think maybe what you could say is that all of the work, both stylistically and thematically, has this sense of accumulation where either the viewer or the characters, as in **Bubblegum**, are trying to resist the monotony which is set upon them, or simply succumb to it as a blissful denial. It's what I like about Kafka and Walser and that whole Eastern European thing about work, work, work and ritual and how you either try and conform to it, or slip out. To me both are just as fascinating and that's what I want to explore for this Greek film.

JS: Finally, weren't you arrested in New York, can you elaborate on the sordid details for the people reading this?

PS: I just happened to fall in with the wrong crowd. It was my first time in America and I just found my way around by hanging out with my cousin and his friends in Queens and Brooklyn. All they did was take drugs every waking hour, and wander round the streets all night trying to score. I got caught up in all that, and ended up getting arrested in a stolen car just after they'd scored. These things happen. I knew that the guy I was with did time for murder and had a gun in the car, only I didn't know the car was stolen. Luckily the police never found the gun or the weed, and we ended up having quite a pleasant joint in the cell, along with our sandwiches. They kept us locked up for twenty four hours in Brooklyn's detention center, then I got community service a week after, though I managed to get out of it. It was a great introduction to New York.

[1] Otter has worked primarily in the field of performance art based on sexuality/sex. Her performances vary from extreme manifestations of sado-masochism through to subversive burlesque.

[2] Located in Kings Cross, London, the now-defunct Scala was one of the most important cinemas in the capital. The Scala defied censorship by screening: queer cinema, bizarre pornography, weird art films, and neglected B movies, as well as rarely screened cinematic classics. Besides screening films the Scala also hosted now-legendary nights by Industrial Records (Throbbing Gristle, Monte Cazzaza, and Leather Nun), Jorg Buttgereit, Richard Kern, Nick Cave, Lydia Lunch, and Gallon Drunk, amongst many others.

[3] Andrei Tarkovsky directed, amongst others, *Solaris* (1972), *Stalker* (1979), and *The Sacrifice* (1986).

[4] Aki Kauismaki directed *Ariel* (1989), *Lenningrad Cowboys Go America* (1989). and *La Vie de Boheme* (1993).

[5] Luis Bunuel collaborated with artist Salvador Dali on *Un Chien Andalou* (1928) and *L'Age D'Or* (1930). Bunuel's life long carrier in film included the direction of such classics as *Le Mort en la Jardin* (1956), *The Exterminating Angel* (1962), and *Simon Of The Desert* (1966).

[6] Richard Kern was a key 'member' of the Cinema of Transgression 'movement', and directed, amongst others, *Fingered* (1986) and *Submit To Me Now* (1988). He currently works as a photographer. (See Jack Sargeant: *Deathtripping: The Cinema Of Transgression*, Creation Books, 1995).

[7] One of the first underground filmmakers, who continually experimented in both subject matter and style, Stan Brackhage directed *Anticipation Of The Night* (1958), *Window Water Baby Moving* (1959), *Dog Star Man* (1959/64) and many others.

[8] Michael Snow is a visual artist and musician. In the fifties he worked as a jazz musician. In the early sixties he began working on a series of paintings called Walking Women. He directed various short films, including: *Wavelength* (1966/7) and *Back And Forth* (1969), like his paintings these films were concerned with light and colour, an interest in part stimulated by the blinding of his father when Snow was fifteen.

[9] Directed by Jack Smith in 1963, *Flaming Creatures* remains one of the most exciting underground films made, with its depiction of heterogenous, poly-morphically perverse sexuality the film was the subject of censorship and prosecution. (See Jack Sargeant, *Naked Lens: Beat Cinema*, Creation Books, 1997)

[10] LaMonte Young began his musical career in the fifties, playing saxophone with musicians such as Don Cherry. Following a move to New York, Young began experimenting with the extension of musical time duration, forming – in 1962 – the looseknit group The Theatre Of Eternal Music with Tony Conrad, Marian Zazeela, Angus Maclise and John Cale, both of whom would later utilise these experimental ideas in the Velvet Underground. LaMonte Young and Marian Zazeela began to experiment with creating dream houses; site specific installations in which light and sound would be

played continually, creating total environments, they continue to work with sound and light today.

[11] Steve Reich was one of the founding figures of minimalism, inspired by the 12th Century composer Peroth, and American composer Terry Riley. Reich began composing music using tape loops of sections of intoned dialogue created by human voices (i.e 'It's Gonna Rain').

[12] Philip Glass is viewed as a founding figure in minimalism, although he rejects the term, believing his work is "music with repetitive stretches". Glass composed the opera *Einstein On The Beach* with theatrical experimenter Robert Wilson in 1976. He is probably best known for his scores for films such as *Koyaanisqatsi* (Godfrey Reggio, 1983), *Mishima: A Life In Four Chapters* (Paul Schrader, 1985) and *Candyman* (Bernard Rose, 1992) amongst others.

[13] Tony Conrad began as an experimental minimalist composer, writing pieces such as 'Three Loops For Performers And Tape Recorders' (1961). Conrad became interested in creating music based on long durations of perfect pitch, creating a sustained drone. He worked with The Theatre Of Eternal Music, as well as the Dream Syndicate (whose members where the same as those of Young's group). Between 1962 - 1964 Conrad lived at 56 Ludlow Street, New York, where he shared an apartment with, at various times, both Jack Smith and John Cale, and it was natural that his sonic experiments would cross with the performance, theatrical, and cinematic interests of Jack Smith, for whom Conrad would compile/construct the soundtrack for *Flaming Creatures*. In 1965 Conrad directed *The Flicker*, a film of flickering black and white, which explores a zone similar to his musical experiments. Conrad continues to compose and experiment with music.

[14] *Dorothy, The Kansas City Pothead*, was a film-as-prank constructed by John Waters in 1966/7.

[15] Ed Wood has become increasingly well known, following the release of Tim Burton's bio-pic *Ed Wood* (1994). Wood existed outside of the miasma of Hollywood, preferring instead to pursue his own unique visions, in the process he directed such classics as *Glen Or Glenda?* (1953), *Plan 9 From Outer Space* (1956), and *Night Of The Gouls* (1960).

Aural Celluloid

Ten Brief Notes and Observations on Underground Film and Underground Music

The following annotated list is merely the tip-of-the-iceberg of interactions between practitioners of subcultural music and producers of underground film. There are, of course, literally, hundreds of other films, all of which are of an equally importance. The following, presented in a superficially chronological order, are, thus, merely suggestions for starting points for zones of further research.

1. Harry Smith – underground maestro, and animator of alchemical transmogrifications, used his silent film No. 2 (1940 - 42) – part of his numerically titled series commonly referred to as his Early Abstractions – and edited the hand-painted celluloid to Dizzy Gillespie's 'Gracho Guero'. The music and film combined to create a gesture that various Beats (most notably Allen Ginsberg who later became a close friend of Smith's) perceived – and described as – transcendental. The swirling chaos that characterised Smith's life (he was itinerant for periods of time, staying at various notorious New York hotels, and there are numerous stories about his deliberate destruction of his films) sucked this print into a vortex where it vanished, and was presumed to be lost. Other prints were 'updated' by Smith, who replaced the original be-bop soundtrack – and scored all of his Early Abstractions – with the entire Beatles' first album. A print, which may be the Gillespie scored, missing-presumed-lost version was re-discovered by Smith's protegee M. Henry Jones in the Autumn of 1997.

2. Kenneth Anger – like Smith a magus, philosopher and filmmaker of epic proportions – scored his queer hymn to leather clad speed freak biker boys – *Scorpio Rising* (1963) – with a selection of, predominantly, girl group pop songs. Images, colours, and textures danced across the film following the rhythms, themes, and pure, raw, sexuality of the songs. Anger's able manipulation of both film and extra-diagetic soundtrack remains vastly influential in dominant modes of cinema, see, for example, David Lynch, Martin Scorsese, as well as helping to inform the concept of the music video.

3. Shot on outdated and overexposed film, *Flaming Creatures* (1963) is a

Set-up for Expanded Cinema performance of 'Elegy' on Tzadik tour, 1997

testament to desire, Jack Smith's film not only used a brief selection of obscure pop songs (including the Latin pop songs Amapola and Siboney) in its collage soundtrack, but, more importantly, was one of the first films to recognize the vertiginous thrill of the gender transgressive acts of camp and drag. In Smith's film heterogenous creatures suck, fuck, and party as the world ends. The film's geist is rock: loud, nasty, shocking, perverse, resoundingly other, and – most importantly – fun. Members of the cast would go on to work within the field of Queer Theatre, and subsequently have a vast influence on both glitter rock and New York punk.

4. Andy Warhol's films – and especially his films produced prior to his work with Paul Morrissey – embraced the radical sexual underground, the avant garde, and the drug scene, as well as New York's hipsters and beautiful (and frequently dysfunctional) people. Warhol's early movies (such as **Kiss**, 1963, and his series of numbered **Screen Test** films, 1965) were often silent, and were screened with live accompaniment from the Velvet Underground, under the collective title The Exploding Plastic Inevitable. These multi-media expanded cinema performances presented underground film and live music as indelibly linked, and inspired both musicians and filmmakers alike in an allegiance that continues within the underground.

5. John Waters' entire ouvre is based, at least partly, on an appreciation of crime, delinquency rebellion, B movies, excitement, early pop music and rock and roll. With his Little Richard moustache, Waters symbolises that most

important of rock and roll trait: pure attitude and a sneering contempt for the dull. Probably his most rock and roll movie was **Pink Flamingoes** (1972) - the first of his trash trilogy — which, with its celebration of the outsider and the gang, a group of pre-punk punks – ostensibly presented the rebellious lifestyle as the definitive lifestyle. The film also contains that most ultimate of soundtrack accompaniments: a pink puckering asshole miming Surfin' Bird.

6. The English filmmaker, queer activist, magikal gardener, and - following his cannonisation by the Sisters of Perpetual Indulgence – Saint, Derek Jarman repeatedly worked with musicians, but one of the most interesting of these interactions was realized in **TG: Psychic Rally In Heaven** (1977). In this short film Jarman presents a super 8 documentation which goes beyond any classic notions of representation of an event and into the realm of hypnogogia – the celluloid image emerges as pure interpretative form and colour, rather than merely a portrayal of the musicians. The film is both a visual compliment to Throbbing Gristle's pure-sound experimentation, and simultaneously a step beyond that sound, into the director's personal realm of the magikal.

7. Emerging from Downtown New York in the late seventies (circa 1977), the filmmakers subsequently described – somewhat broadly – as 'No Wave' worked extensively with the musicians of the similarly named post-punk genre. Directors such as Beth & Scott B, Amos Poe, James Nares, Vivienne Dick, and – later – Nick Zedd, Richard Kern, Tommy Turner and Casandra Stark collaborated and cast their films with No Wave and post-punk / downtown musicians such as Teenage Jesus's Lydia Lunch, The Lounge Lizard's John Lurie, DNA's Arto Lindsay, and Richard Hell amongst others. The films that these directors produced - such as (respectively) **Black Box** (1978), **Subway Riders** (1981), **Rome 78** (1978), **She Had Her Gun Already** (1978), **Geek Maggot Bingo** (1983), **Fingered** (1986), **Where Evil Dwells** (1985), and **Dead On My Arm** (1985), shared with the musicians and bands an aesthetic which embraced: extremity, confrontation, and the desire to produce concise and immediate statements.

8. *Siesan* (1990) depicts a young, uniformed, Japanese woman, who removes her clothes to reveal white panties, she then uses a ritual knife to commit Harakiri. Directed by Japanese noise ubermensch Masami Akita (aka Merzbow), with the assistance of Chimuo Nireki and the Kinbiken club, this film follows the same extreme sadomasochistic sexual obsessions as Merzbow's music. In *Siesan*, and his subsequent forays into video, Masami Akita reveals that he is one of the few musicians who is as skilled in working with the medium of film in order to document his obsessions, as he is with sound, and is as able to catalogue his obsessions with power and conviction in both arts.

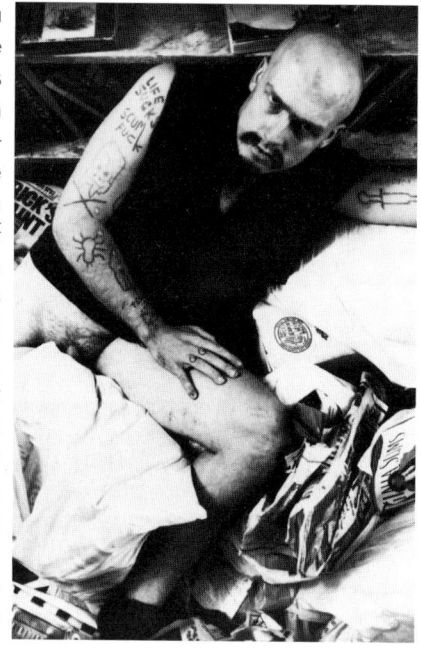

G.G.Allin in **Hated: G.G.Allin & the Murder Junkies**, 1993
Photo by R.Kern

9. *Hated: GG Allin And The Murder Junkies* (1993), directed by Todd Phillips and produced by Andrew Gurland, this underground documentary follows the confrontational punk performer GG Allin. Renown for, amongst other acts of punk-warfare, announcing his ambition of an onstage suicide, beating up members of the audience, and scoffing down his own shit midsong, the film combines interviews with GG, members of his band, teachers, associates, and fans. *Hated* simultaneously explores the motivations of the powder-keg performer, while also engaging in a similarly salacious voyeuristic freak-show thrill as the mondo movie genre.

10. Tessa Hughes-Freeland and Ela Troyano's *Eulogy For Jean Genet* (1994 - 97) takes the expanded cinema proposed by The Exploding Plastic Inevitable to new potentialities, written in collaboration with the master of musical bricolage, John Zorn, it is one of the best examples of the multi-media experience. To Hughes-Freeland and Troyano film itself is manifested as music, and via multiple projections, the use of coloured glass, filters, toys, mirrors, and loops, they `jam' with film – utilizing both original and found footage - in a manner analogous to free-music. Their expanded cinema pieces have the syncopation, and freedom of jazz, as images soar and fall, riff, repeat, and rock. Note, in addition, that they toured *Eulogy* through some of the grungier-rock clubs of Europe and America, and presented the film in a night club/performance context as music.

Tessa Hughes Freeland & Ela Troyano performing Expanded Cinema performance

The underground film and music scene still exist in a symbiotic relationship, with musicians frequently providing original scores for films, see, for example: Michelle Handelman's *Blood Sisters* (1991) which features an original score by Frightwig, who reformed in order to work on the film, or Jim Sikora's *Walls*

In The City, the musical arrangements of which were so successful the musicians who scored the film later became the Dennisen Kimbel Trio. Musician's also regularly appear in underground films, and several films feature a cameo from at least one willing musician, for example Sarah Jacobson's ***Mary Jane's Not A Virgin Anymore*** (1996) features an appearance by Jello Biafra (Dead Kennedy's), or Raymond Pettibon's film ***The Whole World Is Watching – Weathermen '69*** (1989) which features appearances from Sonic Youth's Kim Gordon and Thurston Moore. Such collaborations can only ever be fruitful, demanding that both parties cross boundaries, and explore the nature of working within other fields, and subsequently exploring their own artistic practice within a new context.

Tracing the Edge Of Power:

A Brief Introduction to the Film And Art Of Beth B.

"Communication and information are power" – Beth B. *Day Of Hope*, November, 1992.

The central thematic of Beth B's work, as filmmaker, sculptor, artist, and writer is power. Through a wide range of texts, Beth B has attempt to trace out the various manifestations of power which construct the experiences of 'individuals' and communities predominantly, although not exclusively, in contemporary Western society. Power, as it is described throughout B's work, is a flux of forces, emerging from a complex web of relationships from which there is no possible escape to an external zone. Power does not merely control people, nor does it necessarily come 'down from above' as modus operandi of the oppressive state, although this form of state power is, undoubtedly, a feature of B's work, B also traces out the relationship between 'individuals' and power. This relationship can take various forms; such as sadomasochism (sexual and social) with the continual exchanges of power inherent in such relationships, the willing acquiescence of personal freedoms to the power of narcotic addiction, and the reoccurring abuses transpiring within the very psyche of the 'normal' family. In addition to this exploration of power over the 'individual', B's work also demands that the subject constructed by and through narratives of power can take control via an investment of power within their own daily existence, their own body, their own community. The questions and demands of empowerment - as a survival strategy – are as much B's themes as the negative oppressive forms of power.

"The moment you are born somebody has power over you. [It] is part of our existence from the day we are born, and it influences our lives in every aspect....You have to end up dealing with certain kinds of power relationships and it has been something, feeling like I am coming into adulthood at this late stage of my life, realizing I have choices about what I want to do and what I don't want to do, who I'm going to be, who I am going to allow into my life or in my work, or whatever. It still has to do with control and how much I want to control something or don't want to control it."

Bob Mason in *Black Box*
©1979 Beth B & Scott B

These explorations of power are played out in Beth B's work through the recurrent usage of themes such as; addiction, sexuality, violence, mind-control, discipline and punishment, mental illness, and familial abuse. The presentation of power within B's work is never simplistic and resists offering dialectical solutions, and this unwillingness on B's part to either preach or explain – an act which would make the artist into a new authority figure and hence encourage the audience's disempowerment, has resulted, especially early on in her career, in misunderstandings of her work and accusations of being beholden to power.

Beth B grew up in the sixties on the South Side of Chicago, where she was influenced by "guys with cigarettes hanging out of their mouths, and women with ratted bouffant hairdos; it was the dark side that fascinated me, the poor white trash that I always felt in life with"[1]. The neighbourhood, and more importantly the street, was where life could be experienced; where philosophies and behaviors which existed contra to those of mainstream society could be played out. The street acts as a site in which information can be presented – and taken in – as raw experience, with an immediacy which remains unmediated by the traditional barriers of 'good taste', and 'value'. As much of B's work reveals, the street, and the normally hidden 'dark side' still hold a fascination for her, as both a source of inspiration and as a zone in which to operate (see below).

Beth B was encouraged in the arts from an early age, initially studying at the Art Institute of Chicago as a child. An experience she was later to consolidate by studying at the University of California at Irvine, and the School of Visual Arts, New York. While studying at the School of Visual Arts, B was able to take a year study abroad, this enabled her to study in Holland and Germany, where she worked for three months as Assistant Curator at the Ingrid Oppenheim Gallery. This experience of the 'art world' left Beth B feeling "frustrated with the state of the arts" and, on returning to New York, she decided to begin filmmaking, and began to co-direct a series of super 8 movies. This antagonism to the "fine arts in particular" was due to the limited, and perhaps exclusive, audience that the fine arts reached. In contrast to this, film offered a method of communication which would enable a larger, and more diverse, audience to be reached.

Beth B's first six films were collaborations with Scott B, the initial 'B' served to signify a shared interest in low budget B-movies, and their 'generic'/'populist' aesthetic of sex, violence and melodrama, the name also, undoubtedly, reflected the punk minimalism of the time. The B's were part of the re-birth of New York underground film, which also saw similarly punk influenced super-8 films being produced by Vivienne Dick (*Beauty Becomes The Beast*, 1979), Amos Poe (*Blank Generation*, 1976), Michael Oblowitz (*X-Terminator*, 1979), and James Nares (*Rome '78*, 1978), among others. The movies produced by these filmmakers were described by *The Village Voice* as 'para punk' film. These early films were largely inspired by the aesthetic of self-affirmation propagated by the artists and musicians of the downtown punk scene, and, especially, by the exceptionally abrasive, nihilistic, and short lived, No Wave scene: "It was during a time where it very much went along with the rock and roll attitude of anybody could do it, so I just picked up a little super-8 box camera and started shooting". The films were cast with various luminaries from the local underground scene; musicians such as Arto Lindsey, Pat Place, Richard Hell and John Lurie acted alongside Bill Rice and John Ahearn, as well as the performer, writer and 'confrontationalist' Lydia Lunch. Jack Smith, the legendary Lower East Side performer, and 'first generation' underground film director, even appeared in the B's work.

The early super 8 films that Beth and Scott B directed; *G-Man* (1978), *Black Box* (1978), and *The Offenders* (1979) were produced on the most minimal of possible budgets, funded from Scott's employment as an occasional construction worker, and Beth's work as a receptionist and typesetter. Stylistically they were a combination of film noir and classic B movies, and were shot in the shortest possible time, with the bare minimum of time spent on rehearsals, the films were 'text book' exercises in the punk aesthetic; *Black Box*, for example, was scripted, rehearsed, shot, edited, scored, publicized and screened in less than a week. *The Offenders* was similarly produced, with the additional slant of being screened as a regular serial at the club Max's Kansas City (the cast and crew would complete and screen an episode of the narrative every week[2]).

Beth and Scott B screened their films in the zone of the night club, rather than the (relatively) bourgeoisie space of the art house cinema or museum, which further categorized the punk aesthetic of the B's movies. The Bs decided that, by screening the films within the zone more commonly delineated by rock music and live performance, they would be able to radically break with the avant-garde cinema's traditional exhibition spaces in which the audience was compelled to sit on uncomfortable chairs unable to drink, smoke or eat, as they described it at the time: "you sit and analyze; you intellectualize". The punk clubs offered a space and an audience that, at least at the time, existed antithetically to the established avant-garde.

The central theme of these early super-8 films was the construction of the individual through power, and the multiplicity of relationships between individuals and various control systems. Sadomasochistic relationships, oppressive state apparatus, and street survival become recurring themes

Lydia Lunch in *Vortex*
©Scott B & Beth B

within these early narrative movies. In **Black Box** – the best known film of this period – a young man, out buying cigarettes, is kidnapped and taken to a secret location. Here he is savagely beaten and tortured, before being finally imprisoned in the black box, a torture device which bombards the victim with extremities of light/dark, heat/cold and noise/silence. Stylistically a punk/noir hybrid, the film merely depicts events with no simplistic moral tongue clicking, rather than preaching the obvious horrors of torture the Bs were more interested in depicting a ten minute climax of the nude Bob Mason suffering in the black box. The film ends with the youth still being tortured, and with no comfortable narrative resolution: he is neither killed, nor does he escape. The film demands that the audience think about what they have seen, and question it, rather than be spoon fed answers and solutions. **Black Box** despite being a work of fiction, was based on an actual 'coercion device' called the refrigerator, the film thus serves as a method of disseminating information. Although having renounced the arts in favour of film, the Bs exhibited the black box used in the film to coincide with its launch. Similarly the promotional campaigns undertaken by the Bs on the street were also engaged with the visual arts, as Beth B states "We used to strip twenty foot, huge, billboard sized things across buildings in New York, with times of our

Salvation! (1986)

film screenings, but they became works of art themselves." However, rather than gallery based art, these were public, designed for the streets and designed for gaining attention, it was a tactic Beth B would return to.

During this period Beth and Scott also produced the 16mm short *Letters To Dad* (1978). A film which depicts 'talking-head' shots of various members of the B's 'regular' cast, each of whom is talking to the camera about the power of 'Dad' in their lives. The film appears, on first viewing, as almost comic, as various actors stumble through phrases such as "Dad is the best thing that ever happened to me – he can make you feel so big and so small". It is only at the film's end that the audience learns that the patriarch to whom the cast were speaking was the Reverend Jim Jones, who – in 1978 – encouraged his followers to consume cyanide laced orange juice, in the terrifying mass suicide of 956 members of The People's Temple cult at their 'utopian' community, in Jonestown, Guyana. Each actor's lines were direct quotes from the letters of the Jones's congregation, chosen by the member of the cast because the phrase related – in some way – to their own lives. Each

Jack Smith & John Ahearn in *The Trap Door*
©1981 Beth B & Scott B

speaker is facing directly into the camera's — and therefore the audience's collective — gaze, the film thus positions its viewers as the 'Dad' whom the cast is addressing. The audience are thus constructed as integral to the text, instead of being 'voyeurs' of disparate events constructed 'narratively', the audience become an 'active' part of the text. Such a strategic device becomes increasingly important in Beth B's later solo video and film work.

Following these four films the B's produced the black comedy *The Trap Door* (1980), and their only 16mm collaboration, the rarely screened *Vortex* (1983), before ceasing to collaborate in 1984.

In 1987 Beth B produced her first 'solo' feature film; the 35mm *Salvation!* (aka *Salvation! Have You Said Your Prayers Today?*) a ruthless, grimly humorous examination of the growth of the Religious Right, Moral Majority, televangelism, and the effects of a televangelist on one white trash family.

Salvation! was followed in 1993 by the 35mm *Two Small Bodies*, funded by German and French television companies, ZDF and Arte. Beth B's most powerful and concise film to date, *Two Small Bodies* was adapted by Beth B and Neal Bell from Bell's stage play of the same name. *Two Small Bodies* is an exceptionally oppressive, claustrophobic and dark film which focuses on the relationship between a police investigator Lieutenant Brann, and strip club employee and single mother, Eileen. The claustrophobia of the narrative is emphasized by the location of the film, which is set entirely in Eileen's house. Brann is investigating the disappearance of Eileen's children, and assumes that she — as an archetype 'scarlet woman' — is responsible for their murder. The appearance of Eileen's guilt is emphasized, to Brann, by her strangely unemotional response to their disappearance. Eileen is aware of Brann's interpretation of her as a fallen woman and hence potentially guilty of infanticide, and she knows that Brann is sexually attracted to her, in part because of her apparent amorality. In order to obtain a confession Brann invades Eileen's house, apparently at will, arriving and demanding entry at any time of day or night. Having manipulated (either emotionally or legally) his way into Eileen's house, Brann engages in a series of complex psychological power plays — ranging from barely suppressed threats to

Beth B

attempts of seduction - in order to break Eileen's resolve and force her into a confession. Eileen, however, retaliates by similarly engaging in these confrontations to challenge Brann's assumptions of her guilt and her anti-maternal status, as well as forcing Brann to confront his own sexual desires for her. As the narrative progresses the phallocentric laws which inform Brann's psychological tactics are increasingly deconstructed. Whereas the generic form of the noir thriller exposes guilt and then consolidates the narrative with a return to order, *Two Small Bodies* plays with the very notion of order, and exposes the very construction of the power plays between the protagonists. Beth B stated "what I found interesting about it is how they... really beat each other down in this sadomasochistic ritual, within this sort of microcosm of the rest of the world, into this place where they start to become much more honest and see each other as human beings". *Two Small Bodies* was screened at various film festivals, including the London Film Festival (1993), the Swiss, Locarno Film Festival (1993), the Toronto Festival of Festivals (1993), and the Sundance Film Festival (1994).

Alongside these two feature films, Beth B has also directed a series of videos, which have been screened at alternative/independent screening spaces, as well as on television. This move to shooting on video was in part dictated by finance, however the move was also a response to working with the narrative structure and length of feature films. The short video/ experimental films enabled B to be "a lot more direct and hard hitting, with more brevity of time. And also [to] explore things...[because] in a feature film you are more bound by narrative structure. I think I was beginning to feel limited by that structure. I think there are some ideas that I have that are appropriate for that, but other ideas that I have lead me back into doing experimental video...". These videos include **Thanatopsis** (1989) – a collaboration with Lydia Lunch – which depicts Lunch going through her daily routine. A spoken soundtrack, written by Lunch, describes her perception of her own geo-temporal identity within the 'war all the time' climate of modern society.

In 1989 Beth B also collaborated with the artist Ida Applebroog on the video **Belladonna**. Similar to the earlier collaboration with Scott B, **Letters To Dad**, the film presents a series of talking head shots of people making various apparently disjointed statements, such as: "They made me out to be a monster", "I tried to be invisible". These build up into a collage of phrases which, as the film progresses begin to establish a meaning and a context. Throughout the text the phrases are regularly punctuated with a child's refrain:

Fred Ward & Suzy Amis in *Two Small Bodies*
©1994 Beth B

"I'm not a bad person". The video maintains an almost hypnogogic hold over the audience, as the faces of the actors, and the spoken statements they make, become increasingly juxtaposed and repetitive. These are intercut with dreamlike architectural images, and brief shots of Applebroog's paintings. As the video progresses the images of architectural landscapes mix over the speaker's faces. Finally the screen turns black and all that is left is a voice, speaking in the darkness. The closing credits contextualise the spoken phrases; excerpts from Freud's key essay on infantile desire and sado-masochism 'A Child Is Being Beaten', the survivors of Auschwitz's Dr Mengele's 'medical' experiments and a statement by Joel Steinburg, a lawyer convicted of murdering his child in 1988. Through these texts B and Applebroog explore the construction of an oppressive power over people who are unable to escape it. This relationship occurs primarily within the family, and is manifested at its most extreme in violence towards children. This is emphasized by the repetition of the child and by the quotes of powerless-ness, all of which are contextualised by the end quote from Freud's text, an essay which explains childhood fantasies within the context of a repressed desire to be punished, thus serving to normalize punishment as a sign of paternal affection. **Belladonna** was initially screened in continual projection at the Ronald Freeman Gallery, New York, before being broadcast on various television stations. It remains one of Beth B's most haunting video works to date.

Beth B directed **Stigmata** in 1991. Ostensibly a documentary, the video depicts talking-head shots of various individuals describing their lives and the increasing sense of hopelessness they have felt as a result of disempowerment due to various events including familial crisis and domestic violence. As the video progresses the speakers describe their increasing dependency on drugs, and consequently their servitude to the monotonous controlling rituals which demarcate addiction. Finally the speakers describe the eventual end to their physiological addiction via an investment of power in their own lives. The recurring emphasis on talking heads, facing the camera/audience gaze, which is repeated across these texts creates a confrontation between the person who is the subject of the film and the audience. The confrontation creates a feeling of disorientation in the viewer, as the shear relentless returning gaze of the speakers demands that the audience pay attention and attempt to understand.

These short film and video pieces were an attempt by Beth B to explore new ideas, and these ideas eventually lead her back to the arts. This 'return' to the arts from film was also due to Beth B's desire to "get back to the streets". Like the earlier move into making and screening film at punk clubs, which was motivated by a need to reach a different audience, so by returning to the streets Beth B sought to appeal to a wider and different audience. Partly this was due to a "frustration with film", a feeling almost certainly borne out of an over-familiarity with the medium, and a desire to attempt to work within a different space, but it was also due to the "realization that the most important thing is not the medium but the ideas I want to deal with".

The first of Beth B's art pieces was 'Surgeon General's Warning', a series of stark propaganda style posters produced by the public arts organization Creative Time, in 1990. 'Surgeon General's Warning' consisted of a series of bi-lingual (English and Spanish) posters concerned with contentious political issues such as; AIDS, censorship, abortion, housing, and racism. Fly-posted city wide, across the whole of New York, the posters sought to disseminate raw information on a street level: "use condoms and don't share needles", "seek abortion information", "homes not hell", etcetera. As B observes, the graphic posters "aren't ambiguous. I was greatly influenced by John Hartfield, I think he was a genius in the way he dealt with politics and images. For me there were certain issues...[and] it was really important to be direct, subtlety doesn't work on New York City streets. You have to be really aggressive." Surgeon General's Warning' used the physical geography of New York City as a space in which to reach an audience, and thus played with the city itself as a zone of confrontation and communication. "I used to do postering a lot when I first came here, stencils on the street, posters for film shows, but also just images" says B., "I wanted to get back [to that] because, especially in New York, you can really reach a large number of people on the streets, that cannot be reached in galleries or museums. The 'Surgeon General's Warning' was getting back into that idea of reaching a large number of people."

In a similar vein to the `Surgeon General's Warning' posters, Beth B edited, and coordinated, an eighty page bi-lingual tabloid-sized newspaper entitled *Day Of Hope*. Published in the Autumn of 1992, 40,000 free copies were distributed throughout New York via vending machines, shops and street hawkers. Once again the focus of this project was the dissemination of information on the streets. The newspaper — funded by the National Endowment for the Arts — contained contributions from a diverse range of sources, including writers (Carlo McCormick, Tessa Hughes-Freeland), performers (Diamanda Galas, Annie Sprinkle), gang members (the united Cripps & Bloods), and community activists (Frank Morales, Lower East Side Needle Exchange, Eviction Watch). The paper sought to erase the differences constructed by society (us/them, black/white) instead attempting to explore, through a series of heterogenous voices, questions of empowerment and community and suggest positive multi-cultural dialogues and "an overall sense of hope for the future"[3]. The newspaper's positive and multi-cultural stance placed it as antithetical to the homogeneous bulk of newspapers, positioning it not just as art on the streets, but also as art from the streets, produced by those who are repeatedly neglected by the majority of mainstream culture, save their statistical inclusions as poverty struck, victims and/or criminals.

Simultaneously to producing the `Surgeon General's Warning' and *Day Of Hope* pieces which were designed for the zone of the city, Beth B also returned to the more specific site of the museum/ gallery, producing a series of installations. The first of these, **Amnesia** (1991), consisted of a one minute video (initially commissioned by the Whitney Museum and the American Centre, Paris, and subsequently broadcast on MTV) depicting talking-heads shots of people iterating statements such as: "they take our jobs", "they smell bad", "they spread disease" etcetera. This repetition of statements concerning an unnamed "them" makes it explicitly clear that "they" consists of everybody who is not 'us', and thus exposes the construction of an 'other' on whom 'our' (as both individuals and as a society) own insecurities can be focused. The film thus depicts the very fascism inherent within exclusionary/ binary language itself. Alongside this short video the installation

©1990 Beth B

positioned pictures, including vast reproductions of posters designed by the Nazi's propaganda machine, which depict graphic derogatory images of Jews and blacks, and are similarly engaged with the question of the creation of an 'other'. Around these stereotypical images of the racial 'other' graffiti details the horrifying list of colloquial terms used to describe each picture's constructed 'other'. The entire installation acts as a vivid depiction of the creation of racial hatred, and the birth of fascism.

Following **Amnesia**, Beth B produced Under Lock And Key (1994), originally as an installation at the Wexner Centre for the Arts. The installation consisted of a free standing structure, revealed on inspection to be four claustrophobic isolation cells fashioned from black steel and positioned in the centre of the gallery space. Each cell contains a small mail box style observation slit in the door, a drain hole, a metal slab cum bench, and a bare caged light bulb. Hidden speakers in the ceiling play a tape of Jack Henry Abbott's book In The Belly of The Beast (read by actor Fred Ward, who also starred in **Two Small Bodies**). The audience/visitors are invited to sit in the cold gloom of the cells and listen to Abbott's indictment of a life both created and wasted in prison. On the far wall, past the cell structure, a dual video projection depicted talking heads shots. One image depicted an actor reading from a text culled from quotes by serial killer Ted Bundy, while the other depicted a series of five people (Nan Goldin, Tomas Gaspar, Philip Horvitz, Robbie McCauley and Jerry Kearns) describing their experiences as the victims of violence (child abuse, domestic violence, 'queer bashing'). Each of these descriptions takes the form of an imaginary 'letter' to the individual's brutaliser. As each 'letter' finished, so that image would fade to black, and the Ted Bundy image begin, cutting back and forth across the two projections[3]. In this video the visitor to the gallery is asked to act as a witness to an act of empowerment; each 'letter' read out in the film by the 'victim' addressed to their tormentor/s becomes an act of catharsis and empowerment to the reader, a way by which they can return the attack from themselves. Meanwhile the cells which make up the installation enable the visitor to experience the psychological entrapment of the 'victims' and the physical confinements of those found guilty of violent crimes, thus exploring the very prisons – both literal and metaphoric – that define our daily experiences. The installation thus serves to create a complex series of emotional responses in the visitors as they both experience the physicality and anger of entrapment articulated by the imprisoned killer, and the fear and anger of the 'victims' of violence. The installation offers no solutions, nor does it moralize, rather it places the audience in a series of 'uncomfortable' positions and demands that they make their own judgments. The entire installation attempts to map out the oppressive confinements of prisons, traps, pain and suffering, exploring the very construction of abuse in contemporary society.

`A Holy Experiment' (1994) was a site specific installation designed by Beth B at the now disused Eastern State Penitentiary, Philadelphia. The Eastern State Penitentiary was designed and administered by the Quakers in 1829, and at the time of its completion was viewed as the latest and most successful in a series of penal models developed by the religious order. The Quakers believed that their 'humanitarian' philosophy which dictated austere temporal management, solitary confinement, hard work, and rigorous religious instruction, would lead to convicts reforming. The regime at the

Surgeons General's Warning series
©1990 Beth B

Eastern State Penitentiary, while following these guidelines, also engaged with a systematic abuse of the prisoner's physiology and psychology, by confining the convicted men, savagely depriving them of human social contact, and demanding that they meditate and seek God. Such an emphasis on contemplation/incarceration/reformation is still played out within the contemporary penal system.

Beth B's installation at the penitentiary consisted of a cell in which the visitors were locked, for four minutes: "some people got totally freaked out... there was a panic button inside – if they got really scared they could press it and get out. Other people really liked the experience – to be forced into that situation, because otherwise they would not have gone in there." Inside this cell the visitor would hear a series of religious exaltations and

Out of Sight/Out of Mind [1995] by Beth B
Installation view

instructions played on concealed tape machines. After spending a brief period locked in the cell the visitor is able to leave; in an adjoining cell they are invited to watch into the incarceration cell via a monitor. If the first cell echoes the prison design introduced by the Quakers, then the second cell, designed for observation purposes, serves to remind the audience of the second 'enlightened' feature to be introduced to make prisons more 'humane': Jeremy Bentham's infamous Panopticon. The installation, in part, traces out the historical roots of the penal system from the nineteenth century to the birth of the audio-visual panopticon of the modern prison. Such an engagement with the histories of the carceral institution was re-iterated in B's next installation.

For B the prison has become a central metaphor, incarceration has played an important part of her work since Black Box. In these two installations it became increasingly explored, as did various other psychic-prisons such as fear (in Belladonna), racism (in Amnesia) and addiction (to narcotics in Stigmata, and to dogmatic religious belief in Letters To Dad and Salvation!). As B states the theme is central because "I think that, to varying degrees, that is the kind of society we live in: locked up. There are so many different types of prisons we live in, whether they are in our own minds, and how we control our behavior, or actual institutions. I just think there are so many misuses, usually misuses, of institutions like that. It comes back to the original question, which is not 'how do we get rid of these people that are so fucked up?', but 'why are these people so fucked up?' A lot of my videotapes are about those questions: 'what is it that people are going through?', 'why is it that people have violent behavior?', 'what is the hope?', 'what are all the different elements in it?' and 'where is the responsibility?'. It is the whole system that is set up that is very circular, as opposed to prisons which are a negative solution, which doesn't work: it never looks at the source of the problem. So much starts from infancy, from childhood, to what you are exposed to, what kind of situation you are in. Prisons are political statements against certain sections of society, if you can afford an incredible lawyer, you will not go to prison, if you are some poor guy on the street you are going to go to prison. It is a system that is completely unjust. It's sort of insoluble in a way, and so for me it continues to provoke questions, it is an on-going investigation."

B's most recent installation is 'Out of Sight/Out of Mind' (1995) which follows on from the previous themes of incarceration explored in 'Under Lock And Key' and 'A Holy Experiment'. 'Out Of Sight/Out Of Mind' focuses on the discourses of 'insanity', and the 'treatment' of those individuals who are deemed to be 'mentally ill', within the confines of the asylum, from its foundation in the Enlightenment to the present day media discourses concerned with questions of mental health. Once again the installation utilizes a reproduction of the site of incarceration; with a construction consisting of six padded isolation cells, each terrifyingly small cell containing a two foot wide bed and nothing else. Inside each cell

51

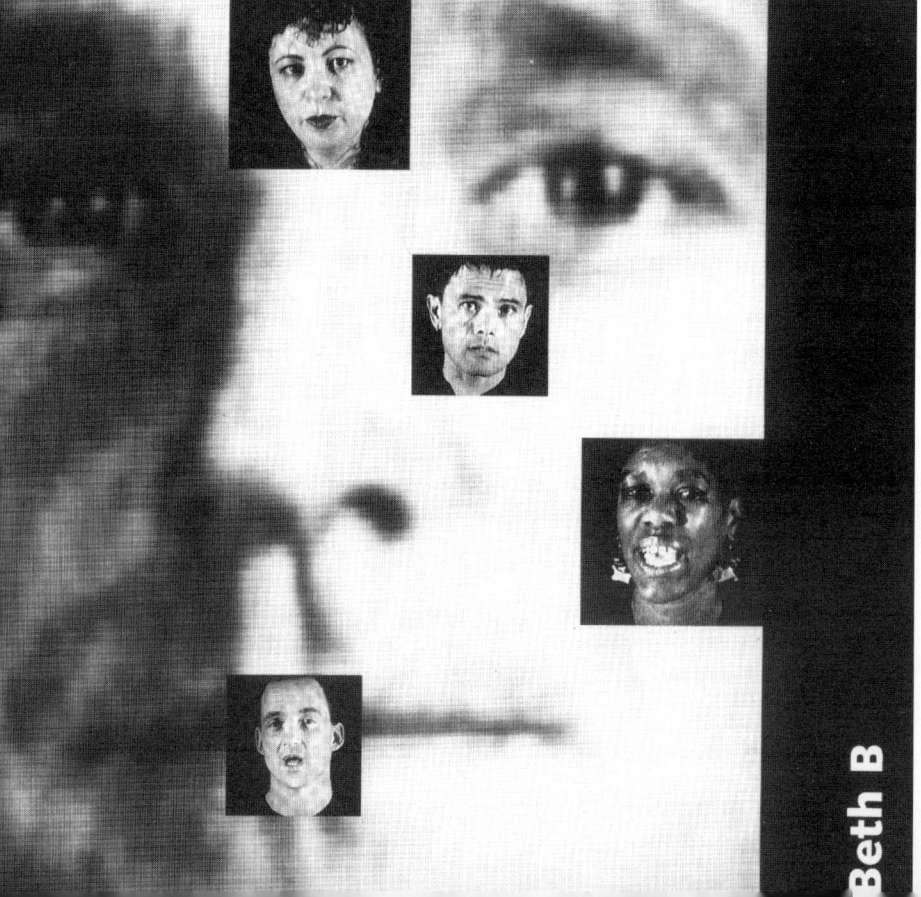

Under Lock And Key from Beth B's video-sculpture installation and exhibition at The Santa Monica Museum of Art, March 1994, Santa Monica, California

concealed tapes play readings of texts by those artists deemed to be 'insane' (and, of course, possessed by genius); Van Gough's letters, and Antonin Artaud's textual experiments. A second feature of the installation is a heavy wooden chair, with vicious leather straps around the arms and legs, it is hanging from the ceiling, suspended a few inches from the floor. This is the 'rotary machine,' a device designed in the late eighteenth/ early nineteenth century by either Maupertuis, Darwin or Katzenstein, in order that asylum doctors may 'treat' mental illness. The patients would be strapped to the chair and spun at up to one hundred revolutions per minute in order to 'treat' their 'insanity'. In *Histoire de la Folie* (1951), Michel Foucault describes the use of the rotary machine as a device designed to 'cure' catatonic melancholia by stimulating the patient into manic agitation, he goes on to suggest that the device was also utilized as a form of punishment, noting that with the rotary machine's implementation "medicine was now content to regulate and to punish". The final feature of the installation is a video projection, depicting various publicity stunts which could be deemed as 'crazy', edited with footage of a body plummeting into oblivion, and footage from television discussing a fourteen year old murderer's 'insanity' versus his 'criminality'. The political ramifications of the installation are clear, despite the veneer of humanitarianism, mental health 'care' is still engaged with questions of confinement and punishment, to be anything other than healthy is to be a criminal.

Throughout all of Beth B's work, but most clearly apparent in her installations, is the question of audience. B's work attempts – on various levels – to engage interactively with the audience. In the film work this engagement comes via the manipulation of the voyeuristic gaze in **Letters To Dad** or **Two Small Bodies**, as well as the use of painfully 'confessional' narratives in Stigmata and Under Lock And Key. In the installations this engagement comes from the direct participation of the audience who are seduced into becoming physically involved with questions of confinement and 'insanity'. As Beth states participation demands "reaction: if they decide to participate that's active, if they decide not to participate that's just as active. It's giving the audience a decision, they have to make a choice. I find it very exciting. But I think that

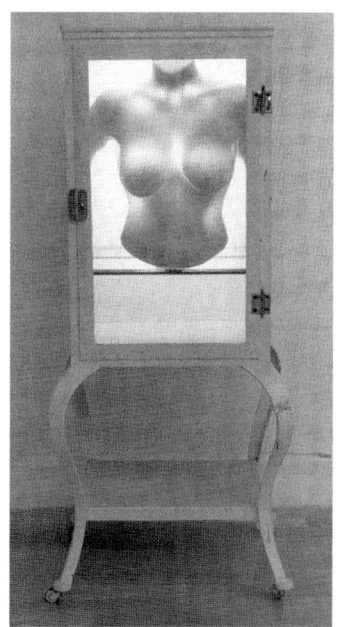 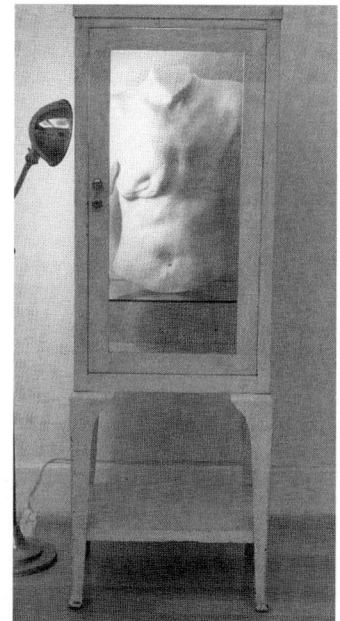

Trophies No. 3 [Silicone Breast Implants] and *Trophies No. 4* [Ruptured Implants], 1995-1996 from Beth B's exhibition at the Weatherspoon Art Gallery, Greensboro, North Carolina, April--July 1997 and the Bayly Art Museum, Charlottesville, Virginia, August--November 1997

participation has not been that well investigated in regards to the arts, and to give the audience the chance to make a decision, especially with Out Of Sight/Out Of Mind, they have the freedom to participate or not, [but] people who are in mental hospitals don't. We don't always have choice."

Simultaneous to Out Of Sight/ Out Of Mind's New York premier, Beth B also exhibited a series of sculptures entitled Trophies (initially at Manhattan's PPOW Gallery, and then chosen to be the premier exhibition at the Laurent Delaye Gallery in London). These sculptures depict – in an anatomical detail more familiarly regarded as the singular domain of medical texts – a series of multi-cultural and historical gender specific body

manipulations, designed for the purposes of 'beautifying' the female body. The 'beatification' processes described by the waxen sculptures of Trophies include; three different – and increasingly extreme – forms of female circumcision, as well as; anorexia nervosa, the skeletal results of Nineteenth Century corseting techniques, Oriental foot-binding, vagina hypertelica (aka Hottentot Apron), and breast implantation surgery, and its potentially disastrous long term side effects (rupture, gel bleed, etcetera). These sculptures are displayed in a variety of ways; surrounded by mirrors, in an old vending machine, and in wooden cases, with brass plaques describing their contents, further emphasizing a medico-scientific aesthetic. Beth B: "I think it had a lot to do with me in my own body, certain things I was feeling and conflicts I was having about my own body and my representation as a woman in this society, and I think that is what inspired it, it was a very personal thing." The sculptures which make up Trophies present an exploration of the construction of the female body as a site on which discourses primarily of medical technology, but also of artistic representation, continually seek to 'define' and 'know' the very 'undefinability' of the female form. A form which is historically constructed as a site of legitimized knowledge, yet simultaneously a site which is constructed as imminently 'other' and alien to all of the phallocentric knowledge systems of contemporary society. This is emphasized further by the sculptures' lack of names, instead each piece is a numbered Trophy, with the medical description of the work in parenthesis. "In terms of medical representation," states B, "I think it's always in that context in terms of what happens to women, because they end up suffering; physically. That is what it is also about; a physical manifestation of a concept of beauty, but it ends up having medical repercussions. It is the medical side of it in the exhibition [which] represents the paternal establishment."

    Through tracing the mechanisms of power as it effects daily existence, and exposing its workings through the oppressive institutions and discourses of confinement, punishment and discipline, Beth B has created a series of works across a variety of media which are the beginning of a potentially vast genealogical 'cratology'. By exploring our own abilities to master power, and to survive, her work recognizes the possibilities inherent in

Trophies #7 (Anorexia Nervosa), 1995
Beth B

all of us to gain a measure of control over our existences. By consciously engaging in various forms of media B is able to reach audiences as massive as the population of New York, and as specific as the visitors to an installation, yet each perspective member of an audience who is able to experience her work will emerge stimulated into thought (be it positive or negative) by her probing political questions. Finally, for Beth B the work provides a forum for her to explore her own ideas and her own struggles, and disseminate ideas and histories, both general and specific, to a variety of audiences; "I feel like, at this point in my life, I don't want to have the limitations of the medium, [I want] to be able to travel between film and art and whatever else I have in here".

Beth B was interviewed specifically for this paper in January, 1996, and consulted regarding the finished text. Other citations attributed to Beth B, unless otherwise noted, come from an interview conducted with her in December 1994 and subsequently published in *Deathtripping: The Cinema of Transgression* (Creation Books, 1995) and personal conversations conducted in February 1996.

[1] Smith, Lesley, The Film: Two Small Bodies, the Filmmaker: Beth B , Visions Magazine, fall 1993.

[2] The film version of **The Offenders**, which runs at 80 minutes, is an edit from the longer serial. A Day Of Hope, Press Release.

[3] A single image edit of this video also exists, with fade outs between each of the victims of violence cutting to the Ted Bundy text.

Screening Transgressive Desires:

David Cronenberg's *Crash* and Bruce LaBruce's *Hustler White*.

Crash – based on J.G Ballard's novel – is a recognizable Cronenberg text, with it's emphasis on contemporary technologies, sexualities and eroticism, yet the film also explicitly articulates (via an explanatory speech made by the character Vaughan) a denial of erotic interest in the post-human hard-bodies of 'cybersex' which were constructed in/through previous Cronenberg films, and for many was their central theme. In place of these postmodern bodies, *Crash* fetishizes the eroticism of speed, soft bodies (bruises, scars, and injuries are shot as images of the 'erotic' rather than 'horrific'), and the glamour of stardom (James Dean, Jane Mansfield, and J.F.Kennedy). This fetishism is best illustrated by the structure of the film, which is almost episodic, replacing the downward narrative spirals of most Cronenberg texts, which, despite their 'bleakness' retain a clearly recognizable linear structure. *Crash* follows a group of crash fetishists through the eyes of the protagonist Ballard as they fuck and suck, watch accidents, re-stage the 'classics' (such as Dean's auto-wreck), fantasize, and orchestrate their own car crash scenarios.

The film's narrative (boy and girl need bigger thrills) becomes merely a frame on which to hang 'transgressive' fetishistic scenes. Key to these scenes is a lengthy sequence in which Ballard and his girlfriend/wife Catherine fuck. As he penetrates her from behind, she twists her head around to look at him (a rarity in mainstream movies, in which women normally have their eyes closed in missionary-position-delight) and asks him to describe Vaughan's car, at one point asking "does it smell of sperm?" and "would you like to fuck Vaughan?" Other scenes include sex with a partial paraplegic, sex in car wrecks, sex immediately after being thrown from a car wreck, sex over the wing of a plane, violent (yet strangely almost totally silent) sex in the back of a car, gay sex, hospital sex, etc. etc.

Yet, entertaining as *Crash* is, Cronenberg's direction retains its 'ambiguous' coldness. While such a coldness works well in his previous postmodern 'horror' or 'science fiction' texts (especially so in *Shivers* and *Videodrome*), here it becomes an irritation. It is as if Cronenberg was attempting to maintain a distance between the charged eroticism that both the film and novel portray, and his own role as director, separating the desires presented in the film from his own interests, despite the fact that drag racing and speed formed the central theme for his film **Fast Company**.

Hustler White is LaBruce's third feature film, although as part of the 'homocore' J.D Collective in Canada he produced a series of super-8 shorts. Against the ambiguity of Cronenberg's position in relation to the fetishism of **Crash**, LaBruce would probably identify himself as a 'Queer punk' (the soundtrack to his first feature film **No Skin Off My Ass** included Beefeater's anthemic Fred's Song [Slamdancing], featuring the immortal lyric "Skinhead guys just turn me on"). **Hustler White** follows the lives of Hollywood hustlers over a two-month period, presenting a series of scenes of various hustlers within a simple narrative concerning Jurgan Anger ("any relation to Kenneth?" he is repeatedly asked, "No." he always spits queenily back), who is researching a book on gay Hollywood, and his attempt to hunt down the hard bodied hustler Monte Ward. Against this backdrop – told in flashback over Ward's body floating in a pool (complete with Coil's interpretation of 'Tainted Love' on the soundtrack) – the film depicts a series of sexual events: auto-asphyxiation as a method of getting attention, S&M torture, a black on white gang bang, a scary morgue attendant with a fetish for serious bondage (played by performer Ron Athey), and the film's 'transgressive' high point: an amputee fucking a client with his condom covered leg-stump.

Hustler White is an 'independent' film, and identifies itself as such with its emphasis on LaBruce as auteur (besides writing and directing he also 'stars' as Anger) and its emphasis on appealing to a small audience (normally; slackers, punks, and queers). LaBruce rejects the purely fetishistic potential of his films (unlike Warhol, for whom the figure of 'hustler' Paul America in **My Hustler** was the central 'visual pleasure' of the film); instead he parodies sexualities and desires, as well as his own role as a filmmaker. For example, in one key sequence Anger is watching two guys fuck on the set of a porn film, narrating the action into his Dictaphone he spots Ward, who is working as a fluffer, on the other side of the set. Anger is so excited he runs across the room, tripping over a wire on the way, and sending the entire set, including the copulating couple, crashing to the floor. Yet **Hustler White** never slides into pure parody, and various aspects of the film are dealt with compassionately (most obviously in its portrayal of the relationships between the hustlers).

What is interesting about both **Crash** and **Hustler White** is that they have so much in common in the presentation of fantasy and desire, and both deal with presenting images of – at least in the terms of sexualities dealt with in mainstream cinema – 'shocking' sex (noticeably their shared images of amputee sex), both are made by acclaimed 'auteurs'. However, whereas LaBruce clearly engages with his film, Cronenberg seems to have taken a step back from his, while LaBruce wants to have fun with his film, and play with his audience, Cronenberg seems more willing to watch from a distance. He does not judge but neither does he appear to enjoy, and, ultimately who wants to watch a fetishistic sex movie which denies its own complicity in desire?

Note that, at the time that this piece was written **Crash** had not yet been either banned or released in England. In order to see the film I travelled to France, where the ciniphiles neither edited or dubbed the movie (it is subtitled). After much media debate – and the predictable 'outcry' at the "sick film" – **Crash** was eventually released, though several local authorities used their power of veto to ban their film in their particular communities.

See: **Rabid** and **Videodrome** with their images of a becoming 'Other' (male and female respectively) as the results of technology, **Shivers,** with the 'benevolent' scientifically created parasite as primal aphrodisiac, the themes of schizophrenic identity and mutant gynecological of *Dead Ringers*. Cronenberg's unwillingness to 'comment' directly has led to his condemnation by the Marcusean psychoanalytic critic Robin Wood, who suggested that Cronenberg's early work was politically reactionary. While this is clearly a mis-reading of Cronenberg, it nevertheless illustrates that his ambiguity has not always worked in his favour.

Louder, Faster, Shorter:

The Manny and Modi Shorts

"Born and raised in LA, Baby!"- Modi

In a New Orleans graveyard a man runs wildly, desperately screaming the name of his recently departed lover: "Rosie! Rosie! I love you. Why? Why? Why?" The camera spins crazy, tracking the broken hearted drunk through the graveyard. Then – a caption informs the viewer – the drunk, Manny Chevrolet, has never actually met anybody called Rosie, and that the following week he was back bellowing the name of another non-existent lover.

Manny has to get fit - but would rather smoke expensive cigars, drink bourbon, and live the high life. But a guy has to get in shape, so Manny has hardcore vocalist, writer, and notorious weightlifter Henry Rollins as a personal trainer...but Rollins won't let Manny smoke or drink, instead screaming at the scrawny figure "no pain/no gain!" Manny is less than happy.

Manny decides to go to the second Woodstock festival. He interacts with the throng of dopers, fake hippies, jocks, musicians, staff, and press, whining in his nasal tones, and gesticulating with an oversized Cuban cigar, spreading non-peaceful vibes to all and sundry. See Manny sit in the press tent, and, in the middle of an actual press conference, ask "Do you see any similarities between this and Rwanda?" Manny dances/drops acid/ screams/gets punched by the Red Hot Chilli Peppers/and – more than anything else – wants to just go home. A caption at the end of the movie informs us that Manny has subsequently spectacularly failed to organize Mannypolooza and – as a consequence – is in massive debt and fighting numerous legal battles.

Manny just wants to watch the football, he's placed a bet and it's going to be his big break, his wife, preparing lunch, just wants some attention... naturally she doesn't receive any, other than the post-game cry of "Honey, you can blow me now". A caption at the film's end tells the audience that she filed for divorce the following day.

Dad (played by Manny) and Mom wave at the camera and push their baby through the scummy streets of Hollywood, accompanied by the song Sonny. Cut. Dad gets a new young girlfriend. Cut: the daughter's party, punks stoned in the family pool. Cut: somebody dies. Life is all but pointless. Odd.

To the accompaniment of various frenetic themes Manny attempts to catch an aeroplane, but ends up at the wrong destination. Cheep hotels and rental car disaster ensues. Trouble, naturally, plagues the three time loser.

Manny stands outside the Los Angeles Criminal Courts Building, he claims that he's a lawyer with the evidence that will free O.J. Simpson ranging from a sealed envelope, to tobacco, to "the scoop of the eighties, a urine sample: O.J.'s, yeah!" The press and public thronging the street outside the court look baffled. Manny hits a bar, gets drunk, and sleazes up to a lone female. He still can not gain access to the legal proceedings so he switches sides to the prosecution, demanding "justice". A lucid prank on the trial obsessed nation.

Manny – clutching his trademark cigar and shot of bourbon - is the big shot nightclub owner, running the suitably named Manny's Place. Here he abuses his staff, insults his customers, and leers at all of the females in the venue. Fishbone are playing, Manny offers some sage advice to the band, telling them how to dance, and suggesting they get another singer "a guy like me, I can sing [sings] Fly Me To The Moon.... and I'm white".

Henry Rollins and Manny Chevrolet in **Pump With A Chump**

Manny is staying at a sleazy hotel. He dreams that he is getting a blow job from a show girl, the phone rings, his pregnant wife is going into labour, he tells her he is in a meeting.

Welcome to the world of Modi, whose short movies (most of her films come in at around four minutes maximum) present comicly distorted perspectives of the numerous lives of greaseball Manny, who fills the roll of the archetype Ugly American. These self financed shorts: *Rosie Mi Amor*, *Pump With A Chump*, *Woodstock Revisited*, *Shut Up!*, *Mommy, Daddy And Me!*, *In Flight*, *Free O.J.*, *Manny's Place*, and *Blow Me* – shot on both film and video over the period 1993 - 1995 – have been regularly screened at various underground film festivals, and have won numerous awards. Produced as fast as possible (Rosie took just two hours to make, whilst Woodstock took two days) the films share a stylistic sense of urgency, which is created not just in their editing, but also by Modi's powerful understanding of the language of film and its relationship to the technologies of cinema, thus, for example, in Rosie, the camera distorts Manny's face with its wide angle close-ups, punctuating his grief with a comic urgency, whilst, in *Pump With A Chump*,

Manny Chevrolet in **Rosa Mi Amor**

Rollins pulls a cigarette from Manny's mouth and flicks it across the gym, accompanied by the extra-diagetic sound of a cartoon style bullet ricochet.

In addition to directing these shorts Modi also works within the mainstream of the film and music industries, directing rock videos for, amongst others, Iggy Pop, L7, the Butthole Surfers, and Keith Richards, and working as director for the TV show *ABC In Concert*, for whom she directed films of performances by stars such as Prince. This has enabled her to gain the skills necessary for directing the Rollins' spoken word video *Talking From The Box*, which was awarded Best of the AFI Video Festival at the Kennedy in Washington, DC.

Modi grew up in the world of film, her father – Ben Frank – was a well known character actor[1], and, as she remembers, "He'd hang out at the counter at Schwabs when I was little and I would take cat naps in the news racks. He would always take me to the movie sets that he was working on. As I grew older my life was pretty much movie sets during the day and punk rock during the nights". Modi did not attend film school, instead learning her trade working on film sets, "I would take any job on movies that I could get.

Mommy, Daddy & Me

Modi and Exene

Then I met Penelope Spheeris[2] and she needed an assistant, so I worked on three features with her. At the time I was hanging out with Exene Cervenka[3], I suggested to Exene that we should make a film together. We both had this great punk-rock mentality that you could 'do it yourself'. Plus I was getting sick and tired of watching other directors do what I wanted to do. Exene and I made a bunch of films together, so I quit working for 'the man' and started to kick my directing career in gear"[4].

Jack Sargeant: You have a background in directing rock videos, do you think that has any similarity, aesthetic or otherwise, with your shorts?

Modi: My music video style and my short film style are completely different. Mainly because the music videos I have answer to the record company and the band. With the shorts I only have to answer to my own creative needs. If music videos influenced my film in any fashion it was how to shoot quickly and get a lot of information into the camera in a short amount of time.

JS: How did you hook up with Manny, he seems to be a truly great comic talent...?

M: I knew Manny from the Los Angeles music scene. He starred in a play I was directing and after each show all the audience would talk about how great Manny's performance was. So I just took our creative relationship a step further and started putting him in my short films.

JS: Right, because, I mean – he features in all of your shorts, and his acting is just incredible, he seems so natural, so I was wondering how much you prepared, and how much was spontaneous improvisation?

M: Each film features Manny because his talent simply blows everybody else out of the water. Some of the films are improvised. Usually I am yelling off camera bits for Manny to do, and some of the films are scripted.

JS: But something such as Woodstock Revisited must have been largely improvised.

M: 99% of Woodstock is improvised. I had no idea what exactly we were going to shoot before we got there. Once we landed in Woodstock I realized that we were stuck in Hell for two days. I directed Manny to work off the idea that Woodstock was billed as this great thing but actually was a nightmare.

Manny and I really click and lots of times he has great ideas or he will say something perfect, other times I might tone him down or push him in another direction.

JS: What's Manny up to now?

M: At the time of this interview I have no idea where Manny is, let's just say he needs some time away from me to find himself and come back to me on his hands and knees begging forgiveness.

JS: There seems to be – for want of a better phrase – an element of focus on the familial and on those smaller, everyday social relations in your work.

M: **Mommy, Daddy and Me!** and **Shut Up!** had a loose script format. I don't know why I play the 'family' stuff with camp and humour, but usually any 'creative' types that can do comedy generally have a good understanding of pain and how people laugh at the dysfunction in their lives.

*JS: I noticed that, out of all of your shorts, one which does stand out as being different is **Mommy, Daddy, and Me!** which still features the Manny figure, as we know and love him, in the first part, but the last sequence of the film, where it switches to colour, and to this more apparently serious depiction of suicide, seems very different.*

M: **Mommy, Daddy, And Me!** I worked a little harder to make a so called statement, to this day I don't know what that statement is, but I wanted this film to [have] a much stronger impact than the other fluffy comedy shorts. So I pulled out a few more film tricks, and a girl named Christen Beck co-wrote it.

JS: How did you get into using the text based climaxes of your films, where you have the 'completion' of the narrative articulated as text?

M: A director friend, Adam Cohen, who edited most of the shorts came up with the idea of the text, and we sort of turned it into the Modi/Manny trademark.

JS: *I was amazed you got Rollins to do* **Pump With A Chump**, *how did that come about?*

M: Henry and I have known each other for a very long time, and I have directed a lot of his spoken word videos and music videos for his band. I showed him some of the early Manny shorts and Henry suddenly became this huge Manny fan. So when I suggested a short with Henry giving Manny a workout session Henry said "Yes, anything for Manny!" At Woodstock we bumped into him backstage and Henry knew right away that if Modi, Manny and the camera team are together there's bound to be trouble.

[1] Ben Frank appeared in **Hollywood Vice Squad** (1986), **Death Wish 2** (1981), **Don't Answer The Phone** (aka the **Hollywood Strangler**, 1980) as well as in television shows such as the *Rockford Files* (1974), and *The Streets Of San Francisco* (1972).

[2] Penelope Spheeris has directed numerous features, including the punk-rock documentary **The Decline And Fall Of Western Civilization** (1981), **Suburbia** (1984), and **Dudes** (1987), as well as the *Saturday Night Live* spin-off movie **Wayne's World** (1992), amongst others.

[3] Exene Cervenka was a member of first-wave Los Angeles punk bank X. In addition to this she is a spoken word performer, and author of *Just Another War* (1995) and co-author, with Lydia Lunch, of *Adulterers Anonymous* (1982).

[4] These collaborations include the western short *Bad Day*, written by Exene and directed by Modi, and including both X's John Doe and Kevin Costner in the cast.

Human Wave:

The Videos of Raymond Pettibon

"We'll make you live the sixties in two weeks."
—SLA member to Patty Hearst, in *Citizen Tanya*.

Raymond Pettibon first emerged as an artist to the general public vis the dissemination of his stark micro/macro socio-political critiques which appeared on the record covers of premier Los Angeles punk and hardcore bands, such as Black Flag (of which Pettibon's brother Greg Ginn was a founding member). Although Pettibon – rightly – resisted the "punk" tag, and his work clearly has ramifications beyond the limited audiences of a specific musical/cultural genre, these minimal pen and ink illustrations savagely dragged art into the punk and post-punk arena, while defining the aesthetic stance of the band, and their record label SST. Pettibon was one of the few artists who was able to catch the immediacy, urgency, and – crucially – the depth of hardcore, while recognizing the essential importance and power of the graphic medium.

However, Pettibon's art is characterized not just by his predominant chiaroscuro pictures but also by its expansion beyond the boundaries of the purely graphic, and repeatedly engages with the space of textuality and literature. Indeed this continual negotiation between the text and the visual is one of the central elements of Pettibon's art. His illustrations reveal a similar lexicon of iconic figures as Pop Art, and regularly include such American notables as Charles Manson and J.F. Kennedy, as well as comic book characters such as Batman, in addition to the mythical archetypes of the rebel, the surfer, the GI in Vietnam, the angst -ridden teenager, and figures clearly drawn from the pantheon of film noir – the hoodlum and the sleazeball, etc., whilst his written text refers to, amongst other themes, hard-boiled fiction, journalism, art theory, philosophy, true crime, social satire, and literature. By positioning the familiar figures within the broadly recognizable frame of the panel, then drenching the image with – frequently oblique – narrative textuality which both punctuates and deconstructs the viewer's relationship with the image, Pettibon is able to expose the viewer to various contradictions, and contrary impulses.

While providing illustrations for many of SST's record covers Pettibon also produced the booklet series *Tripping Corpse*, and the book *Captive Chains*, both of which defined and expanded his aesthetic beyond the superficial category of punk art, a label which Pettibon was naturally anxious to resist. As hardcore developed, fragmented, and changed, so Pettibon's artwork appeared on an increasingly diverse series of record covers, including Sonic Youth's major label debut Goo, and on various releases by Thurston Moore's *Ecstatic Peace* label. Pettibon's work also increasingly appeared in galleries, and was included in the Whitney's Biennial exhibition in 1993.

Since 1989 Pettibon has become increasingly involved with video – utilizing cheap home-video technologies, he has written, produced and directed three feature length pieces and one hour-long movie. The first of these films, ***The Whole World Is Watching - Weathermen '69*** (122 minutes, 1989), documents the guerrilla group the Weather Underground of the late sixties and early seventies, and Pettibon deftly casts the contemporary "alternative" musicians and artists of today as the underground of yesterday; Thurston Moore as Jeff Jones, Mike watt as Gabe Nemisch, and – in an inspired move – Kim Gordon as Bernadine Dohrn. Shot as a fly-on-the-wall documentary this – like all of Pettibon's films – manages to be simultaneously insightful, complex, dryly humorous, and, on occasion, outright funny, see - for example – the Weather Underground going through a record collection and commenting on its revolutionary, or counter-revolutionary, value: "If you're not into Coltrane go join the other side," then – reaching a BB King album Thurston/Jeff Jones comments "BB King – I need this for my chops." Other scenes include Thurston Moore being accused of being a counter-revolutionary for "Fucking like a capitalist," and that "premature ejaculation is a symptom of late-Capitalist white male racist rule." Mike Watt wishing he was black , and remarking that "the white race is a cancer." Jane Fonda pays a visit, revolutions are discussed, pot gets smoked.

The corpse of the sixties begins to bloat with gas. "That's punk rock, by George, I think you've got it..."

Sir Drone (57 minutes, 1989), focuses the Pettibon gaze on the heady early days of the Los Angeles punk scene, and follows two punks (musician Mike Watt as the bullying Dwayne, and artist/musician Mike Kelley – who reveals an incredible acting talent - as the whiny long-hair Jinx), as they desperately try and form a band, and squabble repeatedly over the bludgeoning, yet trivial, banalities of daily existence. High points include: the ritualistic quest for a "name for the band" with Jinx reading through a hilarious list of insane/inane names that include the excellent "Men From Punkle," intense social interactions, and endless discussions re. punk aesthetics on topics such as: throwing a radio from the window at a hippie, the problems of playing a hippie guitar ("this guitar only plays hippie"), and re-invention via self-naming ("I'm not calling you Gun"). The film is a tribute to the power of Pettibon's incisive vision. It was also, notably, an influence on Sonic Youth who took the title of their *Goo* LP from one of the characters.

Judgment Day Theater: The Book of Manson (118 minutes, 1989), is Pettibon's Charles Manson movie, and features Robert Heckler in the lead role, with Joe Cole, Dave Markey, Dez Cadena, Abby Tavis, Jennifer Schwarz, and others, as members of the Family. Pettibon is drawn to Manson, in part, because of the nature of the interpretations Manson gave supposedly innocuous texts such as The Beatles *White Album*, or the Bible, cutting and juxtaposing these varied pieces together and delivering them as prophetic truth. In part the film portrays Manson as a Christ like figure, leading his Family into the desert in order that they survive, yet simultaneously Pettibon constructs a Family who are almost entirely self-interested television brats, thus Manson gives his "children" the Eden of the desert to which one family member replies "I wanna go home," likewise before the Hinman murder Sadie comments "I feel like they're writing about me already."

The film also imagines meetings between Manson and Norman Mailer ("I wanna be your groupie" says Mailer, before telling Charles to move to New York City, imagining the combination of "you and Lou Reed"), Manson auditioning for the role of the Devil in a movie by Roman Polanski, and Manson and Jimi Hendrix jamming together. **Judgment Day Theater** also emphasizes the role of the video more than the other films, with repeated shots of protagonists on the television screen in the Family as Mirror Man (and the Mirror of sixties America),and Pettibon's own complicity in creating mythology. the film is undoubtedly Pettibon's most complex, and most involved philosophical statement, clearly operating on various levels, and open to a multiplicity of different interpretations.

Citizen Tanya (87 minutes, 1989) written and produced by Pettibon, was co-directed with Dave Markey (director of the underground **Desperate Teenage Lovedolls** [1984] and **Lovedolls Superstar** [1986], as well as the Sonic Youth-bankrolled tour film/documentary **1991: The Year Punk Broke**) and starred the brilliant Pat Ruthensmear alongside Shannon Smith, Dez Cadena, Dave Markey and other luminaries. This film is the Patty Hearst story presented the way it was meant to be told, as permanently petulant Patty is kidnapped by the beret wearing, gun toting, righteous brothers and sisters who make up the SLA. Once again Pettibon's dialogue juxtaposes an incisive historical deconstruction with a sense of the absurdity of human interaction in extreme circumstances: for example when Patty/Tanya comes out from her closet/prison she bemoans her lack of a sun tan, and tells the SLA they smell bad — "We don't need showers, we've got M16's," they state — so Patty/Tanya holds her breath until the guerrillas agree to shower. Once Patty/Tanya has been indoctrinated into the SLA the movie really takes off ("You've opened my eyes to Communism, and how.") as she fucks the revolutionary's leader Cinque, debates communism, and tries to work out how to get on TV. Watch in wonder as the revolutionaries argue about the best way in which to share the collective's toothbrush, and as Patty/Tanya inspects the naked ranks of the male members of the SLA and appoints military rank accordingly. Great pillow/revolution talk includes the immortal line: "I wanna die with a submachine gun in my hands firing blood and sperm," as well as the following, during a debate on religion: "The Holy Ghost? How do you get it into your body? Shoot it up?"

All four of these films share a similar aesthetic to Pettibon's graphic work, with the emphasis on the textual, or as is the case in the films, the spoken narrative of the cast, which – in its lyrical density, and its simultaneous status as both complex and immediate – creates the same audience recognition/dissonance as his illustrations (note also that the logo which Pettibon has chosen to illustrate his video series is the phrase "Listen!" drawn onto a picture of a television screen). This emphasis on the relationship, and potential for slippage in clear interpretation of, and between, the narration and the image, is most apparent within **Judgment Day Theater** for example, during, and after, the slayings of Sharon Tate et al, Pettibon's voice-over describes the actions and thoughts of the protagonists in a manner identical to his pictures,emphasizing the dissonance between action/image/narrative. The videos further share with Pettibon's graphic art an emphasis on communications, as the graphic pieces focus on one panel – which on occasion is a bare graphic with little textual accompaniment, and on occasion is swamped with information – so the videos are structured as linear narrative in the traditional mode of dominant cinema. Moreover, video, like the comic book panel, is a recognizable form that is accessible to an audience and is also an immediate form of communication.

The themes of these films equally echo those of his graphic work, as Pettibon dissects the recent socio-historic events that have become the foundations of contemporary America, as well as the roots of the counter culture. Pettibon works with an aesthetic combination of incisive wit, a clear knowledge of the social and political effects of ideology, and an innate understanding of the human relationship to the media construction of historical events. Pettibon's most recent video, shot under the title The Holes You Fill, continues his interest on the sixties, focusing on The Beatles, and is shortly due for release. Meanwhile Pettibon continues to draw, write, and work on new film projects, including a mooted project on Jim Morrison.

Plastic Porn Visionary:

The Films of Eric Brummer

"I was considered a weirdo so I never did fit with any crowd, to say the least the Brat Pack, but I considered myself a loner Brat" — Eric Brummer.

Eric Brummer has spent most of life — bar "a couple of years spent in the Philippines as a child" - living in the Hollywood Hills, Los Angeles. From his mid-teens through to his mid-twenties he drummed for a series of West Coast punk bands; Men In Black, Crankshaft, and Emotional Pain, amongst others, but Brummer's interest was always cinema. Brummer was given his first camera at "the age of thirteen... [I received] a super-8 camera for my Birthday, I always wanted one [from] when I was ten, so when I received it I was so happy, I started shooting films all the time".

Eric Brummer's more recent films — produced and exhibited on the festival circuit - are characterized by an obsessive desire to engage with the celluloid minutiae of every single frame of the film, and by a fascination with the mise-en-scene and grande narrative of s/exploitation cinema. **Super Thrill Overkill** combines found and original erotic and porn footage, juxtaposed, dissected, splayed and visually manipulated via the labour intensive process of drawing and scratching onto each of the celluloid images. The resulting footage is edited with a velocity that borders on the insane, leaving the audience both `aroused' and nauseatingly dizzy.

Brummer's next film was a black and white narrative short combination of stop-motion clay animation and live action, **Joanna Died And Went To Hell**. The film depicts one woman's journey through Hell, from waking in an anti-chamber through a quest for a way to escape. The semi-naked Joanna is led through the bowels of Hell — actually an apartment, signified as Hell by a crudely hand painted sign — by a demonic flying skull, which resembles an animated biker tattoo. Brummer followed **Joanna Died And Went To Hell** with **Electric Flesh**. Driven by a growling repetitive rock-riff, **Electric Flesh** is similar in tone to Richard Kern's **Submit To Me** and **Submit To Me Now**, although replacing the annihilatory sexuality of those texts with a multitude of images depicting apparently unlinked sequences of animated destruction, including exploding heads, erupting guts, and crushed skulls, among others, once again the shrieking/laughing winged skull makes an appearance, becoming something of a trademark image for Brummer.

Brummer is currently working on his first feature film, the narrative *Debbie Does Damnation* (the name, of course, a reference to the `classic' porn film *Debbie Does Dallas*[1]), once again the film promises to combine live action and animation in its depiction of a porn star; " who commits suicide and goes to Hell,...when Hell undergoes a mutiny and the Devil is over thrown by two people, they cut the Devil's horns, which represents his powers in Hell, and divide Hell into two opposing forces, each with plans of taking the other horn to rule Hell. Debbie is manipulated by the decapitated Devil to retrieve his horns back, so he can rule again, she goes from one side to the other on a mission: To get out of Hell through the Devil".

Jack Sargeant: What was your first film?

Eric Brummer: My very first film was a test shot called the experimental film, on the day I received the camera, my first narrative was called *Killers Caper* an action bike movie. My first real underground type film was called *Freak Show* – an all animated piece, filled with clay people screwing and killing. I showed that one in one of my mother's party, I was sixteen years old and my Mom insisted she see a home film since she never seen any of my work, and wanted to know what I was up too. I was the supposed family documentarian in the family and she wanted to see it in the big screen, I put on the projector and played *Freak Show* all I remember was running away right when the projector threaded the film. I couldn't bear to see them scream.

JS: You've also been around the underground film scene for a while – I know you were around when Richard Kern was shooting Fingered out in LA – did you help out at all then, because you guys knew each other?

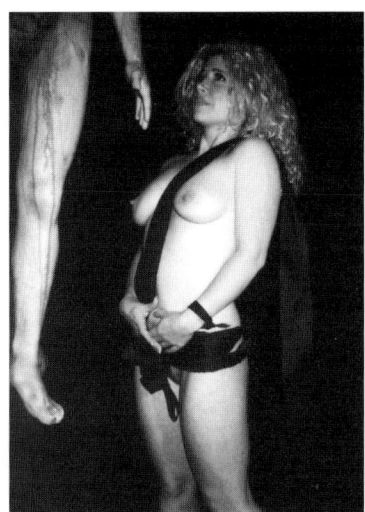

from *Super Thrill Overkill*   from *Debbie Does Damnation*

EB: I didn't know Richard Kern that well back then. Peter Haskell (who played the hick in **Fingered**) showed my films to him, and he sent me my first fan letter, I didn't know what he did until later when he sent me his work. I finally met him at the Scream where he invited me backstage. The place was packed, I didn't know he was big. Anyway, the first time we met, Lydia [Lunch], Marty Nations[2], and crew went to my place for an after-party nightmare. Marty, on his way to my place got in a bike accident, but still showed up. He had a big welt on his side so he was laying on my bed while we where watching my films, partying, and arguing about taking him to the hospital, James Thrillwell [Thirwell][3] was there being cool reading my books in the corner while all this time I was paranoid that someone was trying to steal my Brother's pot plants in the backyard. It all ended when I passed everyone a gun so we can rush the would-be thieves. Lydia wanted to bail, Marty went to the Hospital, and that was my introduction with Kern.

JS: *How did that* **Super Thrill Overkill** *come about? What attracted you to the re-incorporation of these old porno films into new formations – where you familiar with Tessa Hughes-Freeland and Ela Troyano's movies* **Playboy** *and* **Playboy Voodoo***, which also use porno footage – although they fuck with it in a very different way, playing with projection, jamming the film, double projection, and so forth – or did you just gravitate to porno naturally? What made you choose to paint on the celluloid? How long did it take? What draws you to such a painstaking process...don't you find the sheer amount of time needed to make something like that frustrating?*

EB: That film played at the New York Underground Film Festival and Chicago Underground Film Festival last year. It came about two years ago when I found pieces of footage I shot going back ten years ago, plus old super-8 pornos I found in a box, I think I was more sexually frustrated then frustrated in making the film.
    The footage I shot was personal stuff I shot with my past relations and I was going to destroy them by bleaching it out, but when I projected it on screen it looked great. So I started experimenting with the film like a mad scientist and thus began **Super Thrill**....

JS: *Did you shoot any of the footage or was it all found stock?*

EB: 75% of it was stuff I shot.

JS: *When did you start work on* **Joanna Died And Went To Hell***?*

EB: I started in March of 1995, it was to be my first attempt in going back to home weird home movie film making after a six year hiatus. It was to be my first feature, but I ran out of money so it only became a ten minute short.

JS: *How long did it take to shoot?*

EB: Oh about half a year because I had to survive at the same time and I kept taking long breaks to work my ass off in South Central doing construction, I literally had no time, and as you know animation takes a lot of time, at one point I only had four hours in the week to work on it.

JS: *Was it hard working with both animation and actors, how much preparation did you undertake, did you storyboard every shot?*

EB: It was a lot harder working with the talent because I had no control over their schedules, at one point Wendy was going to college so I couldn't use her anymore and I had to animate the ending. I didn't have time to prepare much, I didn't have a storyboard nor a script, everything changed on me so I just threw out my story and used my visual ideas.

JS: *Where did you learn to animate?*

Eric Brummer at work

above: flyers for Eric Brummer's 'Underground Film Night'
below: production still from *Debbie Does Damnation*

EB: I learned to animate on my own, I learned the hard way at the age of fourteen, I animated outside using the sun as the light, I forgot that the sun changes direction every minute so I had this flashing claymation in the gutter called **Monster In Main Street.** I still have it.

JS: In **Joanna Died And Went To Hell** did you design all the special effects yourself, how did you learn to make models?

EB: Yes I did it all, I'm an artist so I just sculpted things. Again, I was self taught.

JS: Where did you get the actress from?

EB: The hard way, I had to beg and plead with my friends that I knew since High School.

JS: What influenced the movie – it seems to me to be a cross between those movies like **Evil Dead** and underground stuff like Kern – what did you grow up watching?

EB: A lot of stuff, my taste would always change – that's why my work would seem to be a mix and match kind of thing. I never thought it would look like a Sam Raimi[4] film nor Ray Harryhausen[5] on bad acid. I was into Wim Wenders[6], Herzog[7], Lindsy Anderson[8], and any obscure shit I can get my eyes on. Kern got into the scene after the 80's.

JS: The sets were pretty funny, I especially like the kitchen door with 'Hell' painted on it, and the idea that the gazebo is some hellish location... it kind of reminded me of the older underground filmmakers, from the early sixties, like Jack Smith or the Kuchar brothers, who shared that aesthetic and attitude that anywhere can be a location if you dress it with the appropriate mise-en-scene[9]... was that a deliberate aesthetic choice on your part?

EB: A mixture of both, I was very limited, but I made sure I got a lot out of the set or location I used. You can take any space and make Hell out of it by sprinkling body parts all over the place and writing 'Hell' on the wall.

JS: What did you shoot the film on, how much did you edit it?

EB: I shot it in super-8 and edited it myself, the only help I had was with the body parts which was supplied by my make up artist friend Jim Spinner who runs Figurative Dimensions.

JS: With *Electric Flesh* you really present a vision of chaos, with all these great animations, deaths, exploding heads, robots, zombies, and so on, how did the idea for the film come about?

EB: It was all just an experiment, the footage I shot was done in a five year period. A collection of vignettes that I have shot and collected with the intentions of discovering new special effects techniques for a low budget. I just strung them together and discovered something new.

JS: The animation in *Electric Flesh* is more developed than in *Joanna Died And Went To Hell*, how did you differ in technique and improve it?

EB: I didn't have time to improve the animation in

movie posters by Eric Brummer

Cinema Contra Cinema

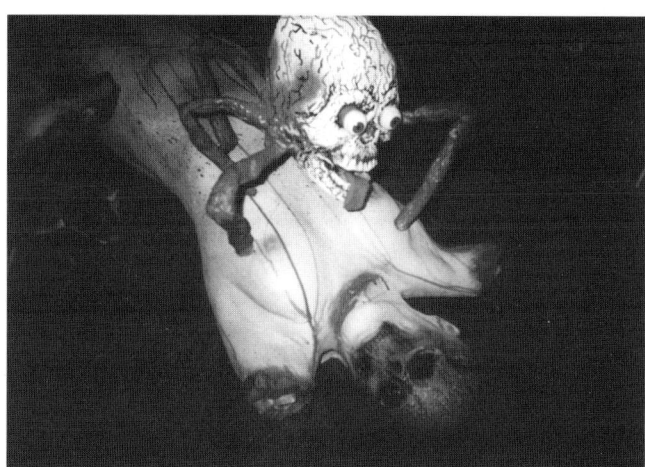

production still from ***Debbie Does Damnation***

Joanna... If I had more time and help, the better it would have been, but now I'm happy with it, I did enough to get the message through, that's all that counts.

JS: *I really love the pointlessness of* **Electric Flesh** *– the fact it has no narrative – it just propels you via this rock riff into a trashy b movie explosion world. But you are now working with a narrative feature length film – why the move?*

EB: Change! I constantly want to explore every aspect of film, and doing something different or new excites me. **Debbie Does Damnation** will be my first feature length film on Super-8.

JS: *Has it got real women and animation mixed in it?*

EB: Yes, lots of women and men, they are all naked in the beginning symbolizing their naked souls, later on they wear armor, it like a Gladiator movie, picture **Xeena**[10] but more perverted and gory. I also have a lot of animation, in fact I'm filming the flying skull scene tomorrow – this thing has been in almost all of my films.

JS: *Who's cast in it?*

EB: You're not going to believe this, but somehow I got that biker actor William Smith[11] and Dukey Flyswatter (from Haunted Garage). I'm in it as well, it stars Jenin Lake as Debbie.

JS: *What about the porn element in it – you've mentioned to me previously that it is pretty hardcore, how will you negotiate that?*

EB: Well I'm going to have two versions of it, an X version and a unrated version.

JS: *What kind of budget were you working on for it?*

EB: This has to be the biggest budget I ever used in a film yet – it's still under $10,000. I don't have the exact figures because I would make money, then spend it on the film, then I would stop if I didn't have it, it's been going on like this for a year and a half, but I'm 75% done.

JS: *Money is always a problem for the underground film scene, how did you raise the money?*

EB: I raised it myself through my job, if I have any left over from my bills. I had a little money donated by a person named Bob Ragland who was nice enough to believe in me. But other than that...nothing.

JS: *When's it due for release?*

EB: Hopefully it'll be done in August, it was to be done last year but so many problems popped up.

JS: *Finally, can you tell me about about the screenings you work with in Los Angeles?*

EB: I started the Hollywood Underground film nights in L.A. and somehow it's growing really big, but politics is now playing into our shows because of content. Again, I don't really understand this rating thing, but just because we sometimes show films that are not for the squeamish, the establishment would question our motives and make it harder for us to do a show by upping the rental price at their venue (the venue being LACE gallery-but they want it to be called the Black Box Theatre) in Hollywood. Originally I started it at the Industry Cafe, I just wanted a place to show my films, and a few of my friends, and it just grew. Recently we had Richard Kern do a show and he was great, he flew over and answered a few questions, I can never thank him enough. I also started a group called the Hollywood Sub-Cinema Conspiracy which have consisted of local artists like Tyler Hubby, Jennifer Cluck[12],and a lot of other filmmakers. I'm still working on getting a film festival going, but it needs support.

※

¹ **Debbie Does Dallas** was directed by Jim Clark in 1978. It spawned two sequels, as well as numerous copies, most of which separated themselves from the original via different spellings of the word Debbie, i.e Debi

² Marty Nations was a member of the LA punk band Crowbar Nation. A long time accomplice of Lydia Lunch, with whom he shared an addiction for fear and adrenalin, he co-starred with Lunch in Richard Kern's **Fingered**. The film was based on events and shared fantasies that occurred during their volatile "on again/off again love/hate white trash romance" (Lydia Lunch, *Paradoxia*, Creation Books, p.95, 1997)

³ J.G Thirlwell aka Foetus aka Clint Ruin, is the musical wizard behind projects such as Scraping Foetus Off The Wheel, Foetus Uber Frisco, You've Got Foetus On Your Breath, Foetus Under Glass, and Philip And His Foetus Vibrations. These various – predominantly solo - projects are characterized by their absolute disregard for musical homogeneit., Instead Thirlwell creates music via a process of bricolage, constructing pieces which mix- diverse elements such as opera/death metal/ grunge/disco/blues/industrial, with a casual disregard for the niceties of convention. Thirlwell also collaborated with Roli Mossiman on Wiseblood, a beautiful and monstrous combination of absurd phallic power and rock.

⁴ Sam Raimi directed **The Evil Dead** (1983), one of the most visually inventive 'horror' movies of the eighties, it mixes the insane/inane humour of the Three Stooges, with the visceral gore of splatter movies. It is notable for its inventive camera work, and low-budget gross-out special effects, especially its final sequence which depicts – in sick detail – the destruction of the demonic villains, which is shot using stop-frame animation. Raimi went on to direct two sequels, as well as **Crimewave** (1985), **Darkman** (1990) and **The Quick And The Dead** (1992).

⁵ Ray Harryhausen was the visual effects animator responsible for creating the stop-frame animation and clay models that appeared in films such as **Mighty Joe Young** (Ernest B. Schoedsack, 1949), **It Came From Beneath The Sea** (Robert Gordon, 1955), **Jason And The Argonauts** (Don Chaffey, 1963), **One Million Years BC** (Don Chaffey, 1966), **The Valley Of Gwangi** (Jim O'Connolly, 1969) and **The Golden Voyage Of Sinbad** (Gordon Hessler, 1974).

⁶ Wim Wenders emerged from the 'New German Cinema' group in the seventies. His films – which include **Alice In The Cities** (1974), **Kings Of The Road** (1976), **Paris, Texas** (1983), **Der Himmel Uber Berlin** (1987) – are concerned with themes of rootlessness, homesickness, and being an occupied nation. Stylistically his films make references to the films of American auteurs such as Nicholas Ray.

⁷ German filmmaker Warner Herzog – like Wenders – emerged from the generation of Post-War German filmmakers. Herzog's films are concerned with the existential outlaw, the outsider at odds with the world around him, and include **Aguirre, The Wrath Of God** (1972), **The Enigma Of Kasper Hauser** (1974), **Nosferatu: Phantom der Nacht** (1979), and **Fitzcaraldo** (1982), amongst others.

⁸ Lindsay Anderson emerged in the sixties, and produced a trio of films in the Brechtian realist tradition: *If...* (1969), *O Lucky Man!* (1973), and *Britannia Hospital* (1982), as well as films such as *This Sporting Life* (1963) and *Glory! Glory!* (1990).

⁹ Jack Smith, George and Mike Kuchar, and many other underground filmmakers, had little money in their budgets for set design - thus necessitating that they produce films using any and all available means. Smith became the master at designing Arabian style sets utilizing coloured material, drapes, shawls, scarves, and glitter (see, for example, his set – built in collaboration with Ron Rice – for Rice's film *Chumlum* (1964)). George and Mike Kuchar's inventive set design can be seen in Mike's film *Sins Of The Fleshapoids* (1964), in which painted backdrops, found and handmade props were used to create a futuristic world.

¹⁰ *Xena: Warrior Princess* (1997-present) is a sword and sorcery television series.

¹¹ William Smith has appeared in many B movies including: *Run, Angel, Run!* (Jack Starrett,1969), *The Losers* (Jack Starrett,1970), *Chrome And Hot Leather* (Lee Frost, 1972), *Boss* (Jack Arnold, 1972), *Scorchy* (Howard Avedis,1976), *The Rebels* (Russ Mayberry, 1979), *Angels Die Hard* (Richard Compton,1984), *Maniac Cop* (William Lustig,1988) amongst others.

¹² Underground filmmaker Jennifer Gluck's films include *Five Hits* (1997) which depicts the results of a teenage girl who has taken five doses of LSD.

Swallow.

The Bad Taste of Sweet Vengeance of Huck Botko

Not since Divine gobbled down a mouthful of dog shit for John Waters as the climax for **Pink Flamingoes** has a filmmaker elicited such celebrated repulsion as Huck Botko in his culinary vengeance movies: **Fruitcake** (1997), **Baked Alaska** (1997), and **Cheesecake** (1998). Three films – each of which documents an assault on the bastions of both decency and family – that have been turning stomachs at numerous underground film festivals.

The first of these pieces, **Fruitcake**, depicts Botko making a fruitcake for his father. Once the cake-mix is prepared, and before the final stages, Botko takes it down to the streets of New York. Here he encourages assorted drunks, the homeless and semi-destitute street people to hawk large globs of phlegm into the cake mix. Huck even gets an over-zealous and semi-intoxicated Santa Claus to participate in the action. Father Christmas leers past Huck into the camera and warns "Kurt, you're a no good son of a gun, and this is for you on Christmas Day – enjoy. We heard an awful lot about you at the North Pole and shame, shame, shame, everybody knows your name, you son of a gun you [phtoow! – he gobs into the mix]". Cut to Huck travelling to his father's house, and the regular seasonal rituals, including Huck's sister who is unwilling to believe Huck has only made his father a cake for Christmas. Finally, the video depicts the inevitable eating of the cake, with Huck's father chewing in. When he offers the director a slice Huck says " no thanks".

Baked Alaska follows Huck to his mother's mobile home in Yellowstone Park. Here Huck reminisces about his last happy moments with his mother making baked alaska. Soon afterwards, she walked out of the family home. In memory of this mother/son bonding moment and their subsequent separation, Botko makes his mother a baked alaska. However, this baked alaska contains some choice ingredients: grubs, maggots, insects, dirt, and particles scraped off of the flattened carcasses of roadkill found throughout the park. Botko's mother enjoys the meal, once again he refuses to taste it.

The most recent – and most oppressive – of this series is ***Cheesecake***. In this installment Huck begins by illustrating the victim – his sister – immediately at the film's opening, and freezing the image on her face whilst he describes his dislike of her: "this is my sister, ever since I can remember it has been her role in the family to lead the perfect life, with a constant smile, the perkiness, the good job, the nice car, the trained dog. She has invented a life for herself without suffering, fear, or anxiety. The problem is that I am not from that world – so this year, for Christmas I decided to give her a taste of things she might not otherwise be accustomed to". The piece then cuts to the preparation of the food, and then the trademark 'special addition' – in this case blood infected by hepatitis B which is taken from the arms of two sufferers via syringes, and then injected across the top of the cheesecake, into the carefully prepared dents which form the words 'Happy Christmas'. Later in the video Huck's sister, her family, and the well groomed dog, munch the cheesecake. In a moment of chilling humour, sis' exclaims her fondness for the red food colouring.

When questioned about his relationship to his family Huck states: "Well, my familial bonds are not that strong, so it allows me to think about my family in a way that a lot of other people would never even imagine. I guess I saw that as a compelling point of view and worthy of movie". The modes of vengeance in these films are specific, and in part are inspired by Botko's peers, "My friend Alex Crawford in particular is very good at vengeance and he has good ideas along these lines".

All three of these films mark a special vengeance against the family, with each victim targeted for reasons specified within the diagesis. However, these pieces go beyond the conventional notion of revenge firstly because the targets are members of the director's immediate family, one of the few institutions which is still largely held in a sacred position. Secondly, the modes in which they are attacked are specifically geared to crossing the lines between clean/dirty and acceptable/alien about which the family most

Huck Botko's *Fruitcake*

clearly educate the child. In psychoanalytical terms the mother and father fulfill a role for the infant in which they are responsible for tracing the limits to the child, with the mother specifically educating the child about the difference between clean/foul, and the areas of the body which are taboo. It is through engagement with the mother that the child learns to be repulsed by his/her own shit, vomit, and blood, as well as learning that decay and death are symbolic of the unclean.

In Huck Botko's culinary films all of these psycho-social taboos are transgresse. His targets are those to whom society expects him to be closest, and the way in which they are attacked joyful extols in the unclean and the abject: spit, bile, decay, and blood are all present in Botko's pantheon of vengeance. Further, in *Cheesecake*, Botko breaks one of the greatest of contemporary taboos via the introduction of soiled/diseased blood into food. Such a gesture transgresses not just maternal law, it also shatters conventional health notions regarding blood and needles which have been repeated as a mantra since the emergence of HIV in the mid-eighties.

All of these pieces were produced on video, in a deceptively simple style which

Huck Botko

emphasizes the subversive nature of Botko's gestures, and position the viewer in a problematic position with regards to the trajectory of the pieces. Botko speaks directly to the camera, and thus addresses the audience about the culinary task and motivation for vengeance. However, the videos are short, and are edited and the audience is thus ambiguously positioned. Certainly the events which transpire in the pieces are real – it is real roadkill, real spit, real blood – but they are simultaneously edited, and thus the films could be carefully constructed. Botko, rightly, refuses to comment.

In addition to these pieces, Botko's cinematic outpouring also includes two other engagements with documentary: **Until There Are None** (1995), and **Julie** (1998), co-directed with Andrew Gurland. **Until There Are None** follows Bob Lewis "one of our most unique Americans" a huntsman who has slipped the noose of society and now lives in the forests of the American Mid-west, where he has vowed to kill every bald eagle as an act of vengeance against an eagle attack on his son. The documentary film follows Lewis as he stalks the birds, and also as he relaxes, enjoying the pass-times of singing bizarre folk songs, and carefully cutting women from porn magazines and meticulously dressing them. Shot as a documentary film by Botko whilst he was a film student at NYU [New York University], the film is actually a carefully scripted construction. The film emerged as a "reaction to the other films I saw
being made at the time. I found that many people at NYU were restricting themselves to stories they thought were 'acceptable' or ones that wouldn't offend, or that their parents would like. As a result, the shorts I saw were generally unoriginal and un-entertaining and unchallenging. Which in my mind is exactly the opposite of what you want to do if you're making an art film. I thought a guy killing bald eagles done as a documentary would solve a lot of those problems for me."

Until There Are None reveals Botko's power as a director – able to skillfully construct a film which mimics the textual signifiers and verisimilitude of the documentary mode. When the film screened "some people thought it was real. I think most people are so savvy to film and video that they pick up the little false notes that happen when doing a fake documentary. Usually by the end of the movie, even before the credits, most people are pretty sure it's fake." Botko recalls that his interest in the documentary mode emerged because "the style came out of the fact that it was the best way to present material. *Until There Are None* could have been written as a narrative I suppose, but it wouldn't have carried the material as well. As a narrative, it would have ended up going for laughs more which I didn't want to do."

Huck Botko

Huck Botko's most recent piece – made as a collaboration with Andrew Gurland, is simply titled ***Julie***. This film opens with the premise that "Julie is a cunt. She is the reason men hate women". This film consolidates the vengeance metanarrative from the food pieces, and also reveals some of Botko's cinematic techniques. The film opens with Jim, who – having spent an evening talking to a colleague, ***Julie***, about her childhood – has found out that her stories were lies specifically designed to humiliate him. Vengeance is called for. Andrew has got a dose of VD – Portman's Disease – which he describes as being characterized by: "itching...[it's] very contagious. This is about me giving Julie the Portman's, for being a cunt I can make her cunt so uncomfortable with the itching and irritation". The film then explores the

Huck Botko's *Baked Alaska*

way in which vengeance can be exorcised, with the film crew involving Julie in the construction of a fake documentary about scamming free goods, in order that Julie can be seduced by Andrew and allowing the film crew to be present without raising any suspicion. The fake documentary necessitates lying, and – as the audience knows – Julie likes lying. The fake documentary within the diagesis of the actual documentary serves to emphasize Botko's relationship to the filmmaking process, and the way in which his filmmaking practice works. Cutting between the shooting of the fake documentary and the actual documentary, the film deftly weaves its narrative as Andrew attempts to fuck Julie and give her the Portman's.

For Botko the collaboration with Gurland was beneficial because "Andrew and I have known each other since NYU and we often talked about revenge ideas. So we agreed to do *Julie* together. It's two people with a strong interest in getting revenge instead of one, so the material is twice as good".

Botko is currently working on two projects, an advert for an escort agency, and preparing a cream pie for his brother. Get ready for more documentaries of visual trouble.

Pulp Videos: The Twisted World of Charles Pinion

Since 1988 Charles Pinion has produced a trio of feature length video releases in which he has acted as director, actor and editor, as well as writing, or co-writing the narrative, and taking many of the shooting chores. His first feature length video, **Twisted Issues** (1988), is set against the backdrop of the Gainesville, Florida, punk/hardcore scene – which it documents – and weaves a narrative concerning murder, zombies, and vengeance throughout the community. Where the video excels is in its depiction of a trio of protagonists who watch the events transpiring in the local community on their television, while engaged with an apparently endless cycle of violence in which they slash, stab, strangle and shoot each other repeatedly. As the video progresses it becomes apparent that this clearly indestructible group of voyeurs are analogous to the mythic gods of ancient Greek and Roman culture, who legend had it, watched over the events of mortals, periodically interfering in order to elevate the ennui of omnipotence.

Twisted Issues was followed by **Red Spirit Lake** (1993), which combined ghosts, supernatural powers, and religious imagery with a narrative based on the conflict between malicious property moguls and Marilyn, the property's rightful owner. Produced on location in rural Vermont throughout the winter of 1992 the video is a virtual who's who of underground filmmaking, with appearances from several filmmakers associated with the eighties underground 'movement' the Cinema of Transgression, including Richard Kern, Tessa Hughes-Freeland, Tommy Turner, and Kembra Pfahler, amongst others.

Pinion's third video, **We Await** (1996), was set in San Francisco's Mission district, and locates its action within the psychic and social confines of a family of cannibals who are slowly possessed by a sentient psychoactive green fungus that they regularly consume. Far darker than its predecessors, **We Await** re-iterates Pinion's fascination with mytho-poetic thematics, most clearly manifested when the family undertake a "spirit drive" – a psychedelic journey in which they come face to face with a gigantic blood smothered grimacing Jesus. This "spirit drive" segment was also re-edited as a self contained short video piece and subsequently released under the title **Spirit Drive**.

Alongside this trio of features, Pinion has also directed several experimental shorts; the 16mm, 3minute, **Madball** (1988), the music video **Body of Christ by Mechanical Sterility** (1989), and two music pieces for Midnight Blue Cable Show: **I Get Ideas** and **TV Is The Thing** (both 1990).

The term Pulp Video was coined by Pinion under the guises of Sam Everlast and Tonya Cthonic, who described his videos as "the bastard amalgam of the Hollywood B-Picture and the xerox machine". These videos are narrative driven, and focus on the themes most often aligned to the genres considered to be manifestations of 'low-brow' culture, specifically horror and science fiction. Pinion's fascination with these forms is most apparent in his references to a world categorized by a combination of animism and panoptical technologies, most apparently via television which, for Pinion is identified as a window/eye onto another world. In Pinion's videos these themes are linked to an altered sense of mind, in which the narrative's protagonist's perceptions – both external and internal – are metamorphosed via external stimuli; for example; in **Twisted Issues** the psychotropia of television which offers the spirits a distorted perception of material reality, in **Red Spirit Lake** the trance like visions of the human protagonists and the emergence of the spirit world, and in **We Await** the characters enter a hallucinatory realm via the collective munching on an alien fungus.

Pulp Video details not just a narrative thematic but also a visual aesthetic: that of video. By mobilizing his work under a supposed stylistic and micro-political banner, Pinion embraces the notion of a production process that exists separate from film: that of video. Assumed – especially at the time Pinion began working – to be intrinsically inferior to film, video is characterized by a sense of immediacy, and also by an image which is more lurid than film. Pinion turns these supposed negative aspects of video into a positive aspect of his work, using the vivid, lurid saturations of video colour to demark a world in which reality frequently fragments, splinters, and – ultimately – disintegrates, before the viewer's eyes, such an emphasis on super-saturated colour is reminiscent of Italian horror master Dario Argento's films, such as **Inferno** (1979), **Opera** (1987).

Pinion's work is also characterized by a unique cinematic style, in which the videos frequently cut to apparently incongruous, but actually essential, close up shots, unlike cinematic convention in which editing is constructed so as to be invisible and the narrative is designed to be `flowing' and `natural'. Pinion's videos serve to challenge the audience's sense of narrative flow and simultaneously confront the viewer with a fragmentary perception, akin to the hallucinatory reality experienced by the protagonists of the films yet without the cliched rigours of `filming a trip'.

Pinion's videos also emphasize his `punk' background, with a heavy bias on soundtrack music by various underground/punk/noise luminaries, including Foetus Inc, Cop Shoot Cop, and Eugene Chadbourne amongst others. Pinion uses music both diagetically – as in **We Await** when driving in his car – and extra diagetically – ie during **Red Spirit Lake** during scenes of ghostly apparitions. Pinion's use of music serves to position him within a similar milieu to other post-punk filmmakers, however the use of Gainesville punk shows in **Twisted Issues** position his work as emerging specifically from a particular local sub-cultural music scene.Besides directing, scripting, and shooting his films Pinion also acts in them, as well as appearing in films by various other underground directors.

Pinion has appeared in Christian Faber's **Bailjumper** (1990?), Joe Romano's **Niagravation** (1995) Tessa Hughes-Freeland's **Dirty** (1992), Mike Kuchar's **Purgatory Junction** (1992), Beth B's **Amnesia**, Richard Kern's **The Bitches** (1992) and George Kuchar's **Furball Blues** (1996). In addition he has also appeared in the thus far unreleased Richard Kern film **Strip For Me Now** aka **Submit To Me 3**. In addition Pinion has also worked as the director of photography for three SM shorts by cult writer and performer David Aaron Clark; **Asianatrix**, **Queen Of Pain**, and **Salome 2000** (all 1997), as well as acting as editor for fetish/anthropological photographer/filmmaker Charles Gatewood's shorts **True Blood** and **Blood Bath** (both 1997).

The following interview transpired in Muddy Waters cafe, San Francisco, in the winter of 1997.

Jack Sargeant: Can you begin by saying something about your background?

Charles Pinion: I was a visual artist, a printmaker, at Syracuse University. My last year of college I started doing large figurative paintings. Jerome Witkin was my painting professor. He hated my work; actually hated is too strong a word. I think he was extremely indifferent to my work. I did a daily comic strip - sort of picaresque hero's journey to a different dimension, called Sherman's Quest. A bus-boy in a diner is actually the reincarnated spirit of blah blah blah. The first day it appeared – in the middle of the school term – Jerome strolled over to where I was painting, and said, softly: "I saw your comic strip." And then strolled off. It was like he'd seen a pile of vomit on my shoes, and wanted to inform me of it discreetly. He's a great painter, by the way. I went from that to studying writing with Raymond Carver and Tobias Wolf. That pushed me in this other direction. So I wrote for a while. And both of them being writers, and kind of slackers, they were like, "Yeah, Charles, stay out of the real world as long as possible." At their encouragement I was, for a while, planning to go to graduate school, to study writing. One of the stories I wrote was about a filmmaker, but at the time I don't think I had any interest in being a filmmaker. I went back to Florida, and continued to paint these large figurative paintings. I had this idea that I would get a job in a bookstore, and be a painter. I liked the notion of being a painter, but I didn't like the garret so much, you know? Somehow I got sidelined, got a graduate degree in education, and taught high school for two years: art, photography, screen printing, stuff like that. I rolled right out of that and began singing with hardcore bands. Many of the people I hung out with were people who had been my students previously. That was strange, and interesting, and I'm sure it helped expand their notions of the way things could be. I liked that part of being a teacher too; I was the one fucked up teacher they could all be fuck ups with. But I only taught two years. Being a high school art teacher is so exhausting, and it dawns on you, at some point, that you are not going to make your own art, and you realize that what art you are making is the art of teaching. I'm not selfless enough for that.

Charles Pinion, San Francisco, 1997
Photo by Julie Peasley

*JS: When did you start to work on **Twisted Issues**, was that around the same time as the band?*

CP: I was in this band, Psychic Violents – my primary band. I was also in an industrial band, Terence O'Doyle, and a bunch of other side projects. With Psychic Violents, I was incorporating writing, music, visuals... I'd do visual things like shave my head and paint my body, that kind of thing.. at the time in Gainesville was not all that common. Psychic Violents was going to go on tour, and we were all set to go to New York and play The Bitter End, and I thought it was really cool. It was only a two-week tour, but our drummer didn't want to leave his job at the grocery store, because he was going to be manager soon, or assistant manager. For me it was the last straw. At that point I decided to leave Gainesville and go to New York – something I'd put off since graduating Syracuse. But what I wanted to do, before I left, was leave a tangible document of what I thought was a vital and exciting scene – Gainesville, circa 1987 – but one that would be re-absorbed without a trace into the humid Florida muck. Very few people were recording back then – this was before everybody had four-tracks – and few bands in Gainesville could afford a professional recording session. In **Twisted Issues** there are twenty bands. It's not the whole scene, by a long shot; it's just the part of the scene I liked. I left out all the jangly post-REM bands and stuff like that. Basically my Dad's camcorder came into my hands – one of the first camcorders, a VHS camcorder. It was the summer. I started shooting **Twisted Issues** in October 1987. Band documentary/slasher film/trip film. On the personal level of artistic growth or whatever, doing a movie made a lot of sense. Jerome cast a long, critical shadow across my painting efforts, while Ray and Toby were incredibly supportive of my storytelling. Since I hadn't studied film, but had

been in a lot of bands, I approached Twisted Issues with a DIY attitude. Writing, music, visuals – everything I had done before separately, but here it was in one medium. It was like: "Why haven't I thought of this before?" I suppose I had thought of it before – for example the short story about the filmmaker – but I'd never imagined actually doing it. Before **Twisted Issue**s I was a complete film purist.
JS: *What do you mean by film purist?*

CP: Art film snob, I guess. I went to a lot of art films when I was in college, and after college, when I was teaching, I still pursued art films. But meanwhile, on a daily basis, I was hanging out with all these students, adolescents, who obviously weren't interested in art films. I had this mentor, an art teacher, who said, "Have you seen **Fast Times At Ridgemont High** [Amy Heckerling, 1982]?" And I said "No, I wouldn't see that," and she told me "You will not be armed with the knowledge all your students have, and you will therefore be the butt of jokes you will never understand if you don't do your research." So I saw **Fast Times At Ridgemont High**, and I watched it without the snobbery I might have previously. Of course it's a great movie. As a teacher, I felt that this teenage audience was basically as vital as it gets, because soon they'll be adults, and unreachable. If you can catch them before they graduate, it's the last chance to pervert them toward some manner of creative thinking. So, anyway, I went from film snob purist to making Twisted Issues. I watched a lot of gore movies before making **Twisted Issues**, just to see what the conventions were.

JS: *What kind of things were you watching;* **Last House On The Left** *and* **The Hill's Have Eyes**[1]*?*

CP: More a crash course in things like Herschell Gordon Lewis[2] and Ray Dennis Steckler[3]. Pure exploitation, whatever that means. Lots of gore. Stuff I wasn't really into. Believe it or not, I still haven't seen **The Hills Have Eyes**. I saw **Last House On The Left** at a drive-in when I was a college student. It was a very disturbing night. An all-house triple feature. **Last House On The Left**

 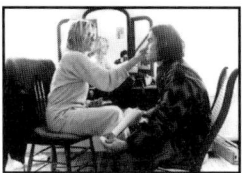 

Production stills from *Red Spirit Lake*

was the first, and I was really disturbed by it. Then they showed **The House That Dripped Blood**, this conventional anthology type thing, which was so normal, it was like stilted, and I went to take a piss during that[4]. And my head was still spinning from **Last House On The Left**. You know, drive-ins are weird environments, the bathrooms particularly. And I'm peeing, and this scruffy guy is peeing next to me, and he's like, "Hey, what'd you think of that movie?" And I'm just like... (whistles), looking at the ceiling, and he says, "I don't like this one too much, but I really liked that first one!" I'm sure I'd still find the film disturbing today.

JS: With **Twisted Issues**, were you aware at that time about underground movies, or were you trying to make something that was like a traditional gore movie? Did you see yourself as working in any tradition?

CP: I really didn't know anything about underground film. I think I was trying to make an exploitation film. Twisted Issues doesn't have any sex in it, and structurally it's like a mosaic. So, as an exploitation film, it doesn't completely succeed. But there is a lot of blood in it. Like I said, I wasn't into gore, but there's something really powerful about gore. It really gets your attention. Just all that red on the screen. While making **Twisted Issues**, I aimed for a high "BSI" - which meant "Blood per Square Inch," or "Blood Saturation Index," or something like that. Very deliberate use of blood, the color red. Red's always been a favorite color of mine. As a painter I dealt with red and blue a lot, partially because I'm color-blind, or color-maimed, so subtle colors elude me. In any case, Twisted Issues is a romp, a send-up of gore movies. There's the shot toward the end, where a bottle of Karo syrup is prominently displayed,

 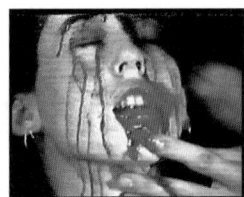 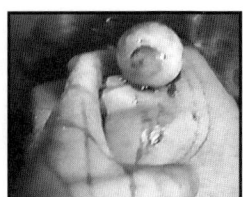

Production stills from *Twisted Issues*

like it's a product placement. ***Twisted Issues*** is also very psychedelic. I can't really get away from my interests in psychedelia, however that's exemplified: trip sequences, subjective experiences on the part of protagonists, hallucinatory fugues... At this point I'm comfortable calling myself a "genre" filmmaker. When I showed We Await in Brighton, one of the questions was, "Why cannibalism?" And my response was, that's the genre I was working in. The crazy cannibal family genre, which started I guess with ***The Texas Chainsaw Massacre*** [Tobe Hopper, 1974]. But any genre is just an armature. If I were to make a Western, doubtless I'd have a guy on a horse. I doubt if I'd be dealing with issues typical of Westerns. It used to be that this was my formula, a more than adequate recipe for a movie: trip sequences, drug use, violence, and good music - or music I liked. I'd add sex to the roster now. Those were the elements that were important to me. Drape them over some rudimentary plot and you've got a movie. I just felt pretty reductive about what was necessary to make a movie. Now, today, I wish I could make a movie as simply as ***Twisted Issues*** was made. Part of its simplicity came from its collaborative nature. It was just me and two other guys tossing ideas around. A very anarchic approach to narrative. [Now] I spend a lot more time on character development, structure, stuff like that.

JS: That is something that should come as you develop as a writer.

CP: I guess so, yeah. It's like lovemaking. You get better at it. But you still want to have furtive sex in the back seat once in a while, you know?

 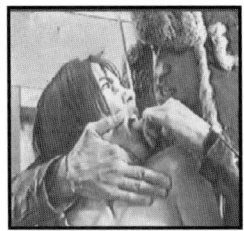 

Production stills from *Red Spirit Lake*

JS: *You have to get that balance between character and exploitation. Where did you show it?*

CP: ***Twisted Issues'*** world premiere was at the Orange and Brew, at the University of Florida, in February 1988. Nice video projector. Packed house. The crowd was very enthusiastic. With twenty local bands on the soundtrack, and an all-local cast, it was sort of like shooting fish in a barrel. The thing about Gainesville in the late '80's, is that it was really like the frontier. Local bands didn't make tapes. Psychic Violents was the first band that put tapes out for sale. Our first tape was from live shows, and people were like "You put out a tape of a live show?" and I was like "Yeah". And the thing was, people bought the tapes. At the time there was this weird timidity, a kind of self-defeating localism; "We're just from Gainesville..." It's kind of why I had to leave actually. Now it's not the case... now you have racks of CDs from local bands, with beautiful Photoshop covers. Just like everywhere else I guess.

JS: *When did you move to New York?*

CP: I moved to New York shortly after the ***Twisted Issues*** premiere. I started ***Twisted Issues*** in the Fall of 1987, and finished it in the Spring of 1988. I moved to New York in April 1988. Within that first month I met Richard Kern, who was very generous and supportive, and I went right from that to thinking that Nick Zedd would be similarly inclined, so I sent him a copy of the movie, and got one of his endearing quotes: "I really hated ***Twisted Issues***." That was funny. I mean, I don't really care for the movie that much now, either. You could put it up on the shelf and look at it, and it does seem like this crudely carved figure, a piece of folk art. But I don't necessarily want to examine it too closely at this point. Of course, I've seen it a hundred times by now.

JS: *How did you support yourself in New York?*

CP: Well, Screw magazine was the most stable job I had, and that was a couple of years after arriving. It's where I met David Aaron Clark. I used to whisper sweet nothings to him through a vent between our offices. Prior to that I worked as a sign painter, a production assistant on commercials and stuff, and I was an intern at Film/Video Arts, which is a community-based access place in Manhattan. That is actually where I started getting access to some things. Being an independent artist in film and video, a lot of the trick is just getting access to the technology. The good part about shooting on video is that it's cheap, but the bad part is trying to find a place to cut it. However, if you're an intern, or a volunteer, you can get access to all kinds of stuff. I have very rarely paid for editing time so far. I don't know how long that's going to last.

JS: *In New York you started production of* **Red Spirit Lake***?*

CP: When I was in New York I actually started developing **Killbillies**...

JS: *The famous, never developed script...*

CP: The script for the Spirit Drive, which comes from **Killbillies**, was reprinted in Chemical Imbalance [magazine] in 1990. Originally in **Killbillies** they don't just meet Jesus, they also meet the Buddah, who they run over.

JS: *And that was what was reworked in* **We Await***. What happened to* **Killbillies***, because that was going to be a huge project?*

CP: **Killbillies** started out as a super8 movie. I bought two ten-roll bricks of sound super8, which were slightly outdated. Very manageable format, and a logical "next step" after making *Twisted Issues*. I started out with a super8 trailer, a short trailer that I screened at a Jack Stevenson show at the Pyramid in the East Village. "Killbillies: Terror has Some STRANGE Kinfolk." Somebody in the audience shouted out "Stupid!" when it was finished. Anyway, I always shoot my own things, but I thought it would be great to have someone else shoot *Killbillies*. A director of photography, who was at the Jack Stevenson show, approached me about shooting the feature. At an early meeting, he said, "I don't think you should use outdated film." I wish I'd replied, "Well, I don't think you should be my DP [director of photography]," but I didn't, and things just started escalating. And then this woman who was going to play Josie in the film got really interested in producing it, and it became a real picaresque tale of crazy expansion, in terms of format and ambition. So we went to 16mm. We obviously needed more money to make it in 16mm. We actually did shoot three weekends in 16mm, and I went $14,000 in the hole. Ran out of money and suspended production. There exists, in this world, thirty minutes of the movie, uncut, sitting in a lab somewhere.

JS: Why didn't you get it?

CP: Because at the time I owed something like $1,200 to get it out. And the thing is, I crashed and burned so hard on this project, I mean, we shot in 16mm, and it just got way out of control. When we started, in super8, I said to the DP: "Look, we use three lights; our characters say their lines; and I have a movie - the movie I want to make." I still think that this is true. Somehow, *Killbillies* went from that simple equation, to... I just remember the last weekend of the shoot, looking with horror as this huge grip truck drove up, and this army of grips and gaffers and PA's started unloading it... it was like a real movie. These huge, expensive HMI lights... way more than I needed. But it was like: my money, some of my parents' money... I realize now that the DP was trying to build up his reel - it really didn't matter whether the feature got finished or not, as long as he got some good footage. The joke is, of course, that his work is lost forever.

Had I stuck to my original vision and shot in super8 I would now have a movie called **Killbillies**. I've got to chalk it up to some kind of educational experience, but basically, once it collapsed, some of the people who had been working on it before were like, "No, no. We're going to get it made in 35mm." There was momentum behind it. So, this German guy, who's now an old friend – he plays Sardonia, who cuts his dick off in **Red Spirit Lake** - became the producer on **Killbillies**. He budgeted **Killbillies** at $1.6 million. I was like "That's too high... too high for a low budget movie, and too low for a big budget movie." But he specifically didn't want to make what he called "a funky downtown movie." Which of course is exactly what **Killbillies** should have been. It became a miserable process. Having to take lunch with wealthy Israeli twenty-somethings, who would say "I love **Killbillies** very much, but what do you think of this title: Cannibal Family?" And the thing is, if I were playing that game now, I'd say, "Brilliant! Let's have another drink!" The movie got written up in The Hollywood Reporter, and on Page Six of the New York Post. Very much as if it was going to happen. Joey Ramone was involved; Tom Towles, who was Ottis in **Henry: Portrait Of A Serial Killer**; Michael Kirby from the Wooster Group; Richard Edson; Deborah Harry; Gibby Haynes was going to play Dog Boy. All these people were going to be involved, it was going to be so cool. Tom Savini wanted to do the effects. The music originally was by Eugene Chadbourne, and then Blixa Bargeld got interested.

JS: *A major movie on your hands that wasn't going to happen.*

CP: Exactly. Propped up by enthusiasm, ambition, and hot air. No one with money had any interest in it. Too "edgy" for 1990, I guess. The ending to **Killbillies** is very Grand Guignol. Tipple is crucified at the end, and they cut out his heart. This whole cosmology, this ritual... He's hung up on this cruciform symbol – the symbol which appears throughout **We Await** – then the whole cross spins, turns upside down. The clincher, for most investors, was the Spirit Drive. It was right out of The Big Picture: "I like the Spirit Drive very much, but... does it have to be Jesus?"

*JS: When **Killbillies** started to fall apart you did **Red Spirit Lake**?*

CP: I was travelling around the country with Ellen Smithy. We were lying in a tent, and she heard a voice that said, "It's going to rain, put the rain cover on." So she went outside and put the rain cover on. She came back into the tent and lay down, and it suddenly began to rain. She said, "Thanks for telling me that," and I'm like, "Huh?" So we started there, you know, a fairly organic process. "Its the story of a woman who hears these voices." The next morning I woke up and said, "Red Spirit Lake", like I knew it was the title of the movie. However that happens, you're sleeping or whatever, and little building blocks fall into place in your brain. The story to **Red Spirit Lake** came out of those clues. Marilyn's in the sauna, the fire has gone out, and she hears a voice: "Don't freeze to death, Marilyn." We wrote the screenplay tag-team style. I'd write for a while, then I'd say, "I'm getting to this sex scene..." and would let Ellen have a go at it. I have to say that many of the really depraved elements of Red Spirit Lake were initially generated by her. For what that's worth. It's my shield against being labelled misogynistic. Basically, we both wanted to write something fast, and then actually *make* the damn thing. Because I'd been sitting in front of my word processor for months and months, working on **Killbillies**... **Killbillies** this, **Killbillies** that. I was dying to just pick up a video camera and make a fucking movie.

JS: It was the opposite really...

CP: Totally the opposite of the **Killbillies** experience... Video is cheap and fast. And I like the proportions of the television screen, even more than wide screen, I think.

JS: More than wide screen?

CP: Well, I don't have any experience with wide screen. If I did, maybe I'd be like, "Oh my God, suddenly I'm in a double-wide trailer!". That's a telling reference, a double-wide trailer. (laughter) I really like picking up a video camera and it's all there. You know what kind of light you've got, you know if you've got an image. On the other hand, the film purist that I still am certainly loves, you know, film. There's nothing like the experience of seeing a Tarkovsky film, for example. Walking into this temple that is the cinema and watching a Tarkovsky film and having that sense of time displacement. Chantel Akerman[6] has the same effect on me, though in a less lyrical way. A woman waits for a subway. The subway comes. The doors open. She gets on. Ackerman's work might survive on video, but I can't imagine watching Tarkovsky[5] on video.

JS: Don't you think that could be said to create some false division between high and low art, the idea that some art should be seen within a certain environment while other art doesn't matter so much?

CP: I think it's a personal thing, in the case of Tarkovsky. Polanski's[7] my favorite director, and I'll watch him on video. It's not about high art

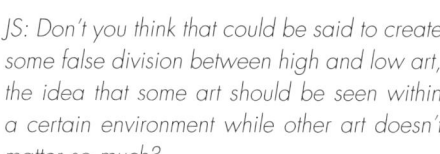

Stills from *Red Spirit Lake*

versus low art. It's about the optimum viewing experience. The experience of going to a movie is simply "better" when it's a projected image in a dark room. I like having my work projected; there is a cinematic experience when you see my work projected. I like the idea of an audience, a crowd, watching my movies. It's different when you're drinking beer in your living room, watching a video, with the phone ringing and the neighbors' kids clomping around overhead. It's completely different. There's a kind of social deportment in the cinema. If you're not sure about a movie, but people around you are laughing, it at least occurs to you that you're missing something.

Cinema Contra Cinema

I don't know where I first came across that notion, of cinema-as-temple, but it's really true. I went to Paris in the Summer of 1981, and the people I went to visit, I kind of sprung it on them that I was coming. I just basically showed up, and when I got there they said, "Oh, we're going to the South of France, but here are our keys". So I spent a week alone in Paris. Cannes had just let out, and Paris was flooded with movies. It was great, just going to the movies, like I was on a pilgrimage or something. I saw *The Tenant* there, for like the thirteenth time, but in French for the first time. It's still my favorite movie.

JS: *I love the ending, where he jumps out of the window twice...*

CP: For me what was powerful about that movie, when I first saw it when I was seventeen, I guess it was the first movie I'd seen where the good guy wasn't going to win. There's one point, after a lot of shit has gone down, when he's like, "Yeah, I'll show them!" He's centered in the frame, and he's walking toward us. And I was thinking, "Yeah, I've seen a lot of American films, he's in the middle of the frame, he's strong now, he's got it together, he's.... [adopts incredulous voice] he's buying a wig." You know, he's not trying, he's not fighting back at all – he's buying a wig.

JS: *Can you say a little about **Red Spirit Lake**, you cast everybody you knew, then shot it at your co-writer's parents' house?*

CP: Yeah, up in Vermont, in the winter. We knew it was going to be extreme. Richard [Kern] was a natural choice, you know, plus he's a good friend of Ellen's. I think he's really great in **Red Spirit Lake**. I have to say that whatever success I've had with my casts, it's from casting close to the character, or letting the character change according to the characteristics of the actor. Often a character will be written one way, then change once the actor comes along. I didn't really have any actors in **Red Spirit Lake**, except for Holly Adams. She was an actress, so she had tons of lines, but unfortunately she approached the whole thing kind of cavalierly, and didn't really memorize

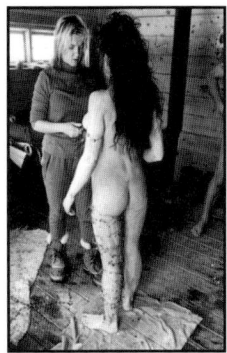

them. I mean, it cuts together okay, but I had to trash a lot of her footage.

JS: How long did it take to shoot it?

CP: As I recall, about two long weekends. That was for the principal stuff, and since Ellen and I were living at the house for three months, we did a lot of pick up shots at our leisure. The shots of each other's character, alone, we did when no one was around.

JS: With Red Spirit Lake, you marketed that yourself as a video.

CP: Not at first. *Film Threat*, who had carried **Twisted Issues** for some time, told me they were going to carry **Red Spirit Lake** as well; give it a cover story, price it at $29.95, etc. They were very specific about how they were going to handle its promotion. I responded with a sigh of relief and began production on **We Await**. Then, *Film Threat* did that cover story, "Twenty Five Underground Films You Must See!" and included **Twisted Issues** in that list. Inside, there was a review of **Red Spirit Lake**, with my address, and that was it. They had obviously decided not to carry it or promote it in any way. It was irritating, but it was mostly inconvenient, because I was in the middle of production on **We Await**, and had done nothing to promote **Red Spirit Lake**. It's like two lobes of the brain, production versus promotion. It was a major shifting of gears. So I spent a few months there, away from **We Await**, playing catch-up. I got **Red Spirit Lake** into the Chicago Underground Film Festival, in 1995, which was a great experience. Something Weird Video in Seattle carries the movie, now.

Production stills from **Red Spirit Lake**

JS: You make – pretty much – feature length films, so how do you go about rehearsing? Do you do a month of rehearsals with people, or just rehearse them literally before the shoot.

CP: Because of the large family in **We Await**, we rehearsed some of the group scenes. Dinner, the Spirit Drive. For **Red Spirit Lake** there were no rehearsals at all, basically it was, "Here are your lines." I mean, shortly before we'd shoot, we'd be lighting the set or whatever; I'd sit down with Rick Hall – the bald guy in **Red Spirit Lake** – and just talk about the lines, his character, whatever. In the script, his character was sexually-repressed, more nervous, afraid of women, and Rick said, "I can't really relate to that," and I remember we were sitting on the set, ready to shoot his first scene, and I said "Oh, you can't?" and he said, "Not really," so I go, "Okay, in that case, you're a sexual predator". Didn't change the lines at all, but it did change their delivery. And to me, that kind of unpredictability is the fun part, especially shooting in video, where the economic stakes are lower.

JS: That's interesting, had you met the Kuchar brothers at that point?

CP: I met them afterwards.

JS: That is the way they used to shoot, if something changes, they'll change the script, rather than agonize about it. I don't know if that is true of all their films, but certainly some of them they improvised according to their needs.

CP: And also Kembra has a good theory: availablism. Which I apply to my work a lot.

JS: Whoever, or whatever is available, do it.

CP: Yeah, it keeps you alert. I think Kembra is a great artist, and I think the Kuchars are the Mecca toward which all video artists should prostrate themselves at least once a week. They were doing it first, and they do it best.

George really likes **Red Spirit Lake**. I'm also in Mike Kuchar's movie **Purgatory Junction**. Kembra's in that one, as well.

JS: *How hard do you find it to both direct and act in your films?*

CP: It's really hard, but it comes down to convenience. I mean, I'm available.

JS: *And you do a lot of shooting, too.*

CP: Yeah, when I can. It definitely makes me more comfortable to be behind the camera. I went into both **Red Spirit Lake** and **We Await** saying "I'm not going to be in this one." To Ellen, however, it was a practical issue: "Charles, you're here, it's one of the main characters, why don't you just do it?" She came up with a lot of the casting, in both movies. In **Red Spirit Lake**, it was mostly her friends at that point, I didn't know a lot of those people. I think as a casting person she's quite inspired. She also cast Tipple in **We Await**, a friend of ours, and it hadn't even crossed my mind it could be him, and he is absolutely perfect. The solution to shooting on video - to get back to that - is this: find a ready-made and point a camera at him or her. For example, the mechanic in We Await. The actor is really a mechanic, who really likes to hang things from his dick. It's not the sort of thing I'd write: "Vice grips hang from Clive's dick." Or in the case of Richard [in **Red Spirit Lake**] it didn't occur to me to write, "He twists the woman's breasts savagely," or whatever – he just did it, and it's great.

JS: *When did the idea of pulp video emerge, was that after **Red Spirit Lake**?*

CP: Pulp video. Actually, the very clear genesis of that phrase was Genesis P-Orridge, who wrote us a letter saying "I loved **Red Spirit Lake**, I gave it to a friend who is into this kind of pulp video." This was before **Pulp Fiction**. And that's when the term entered my brain. It seemed like such a natural term. So I was moved to write this pseudonymous essay, to stake out my own aesthetic ghetto, seeing as how I'm going to be ghetto-ized anyway. Because if you shoot narrative features on video you are in the ghetto, both aesthetically and in terms of who will see it. Maybe this will change, but it hasn't yet. You can transfer video to film, but, even if I could afford it, I'm not interested in that. I can't imagine **We Await** on film in theaters, that's not what it is you know. To me the video camera has the same power as the electric guitar: anyone can pick one up and create some kind of smear on the psychic landscape. Whether it's any good or not isn't really about the medium. I'll admit that it's daunting, for the viewer. Watching movies that are shot on video becomes an open mike night - each movie is a different act - and who wants to go to an open mike night? Unless someone tells you there's an act you should make a point of seeing, you're just entering an anarchic, unpredictable spew of energies. Consequently, shooting a feature in video can be a pure, undistilled expression, but very few people will ever see the result. More people will see a feature film, but it's usually been compromised by commerce and other issues. There's usually an inverse ratio between these two things. What I dislike about making a "real" movie – I'm currently developing a script for some ex-Corman guys, in Hollywood – is that everything is being scrutinized. In the sense of having the most believable characters, and the most tightly structured plot, it's good to scrutinize, but I think it can calcify the creative process. And the thing about just picking up a video camera, pointing it, and saying "I want to have the cockroach enter from the lower right corner of the frame," which is what I want: I don't have to explain it (even to the cockroach). And so I think it lends itself to more lyricism.

JS: It's also what Jean-Luc Godard said though: "when everybody can get hold of a camera the true artists will emerge", and to an extent video gives that access to people.

CP: But it has a technical trapdoor, or glass ceiling, or whatever, because it will still only be 640 by 480 pixels. It'll never have film's contrast ratio and detail. Some of the new video formats are amazing, however, and once transferred to film will probably look fantastic. But it's also about how images are delivered, like if video projection were more widespread, that would change things. It comes down to how video is treated by the powers that be - and under that umbrella I include film festivals, film fetishists, and assorted art Mafioso, who maintain the expensive cult of celluloid.

JS: To what extent is the idea of Pulp Video also an aesthetic stance?

CP: Well, it's aesthetic in a purely visual sense, i.e., it's video and not film. The medium is the message. 640 X 480 pixels coming' at you. There's a flatness, a lack of contrast ratio, some fucked up color things that are unique to video. I was more deliberate about utilizing these "limitations" when I was doing Twisted Issues. There, I made a point of using "illegal" colors, etc., fucked-up lighting... However, a paramount element in Pulp Video is storytelling; the narrative form. Taking the narrative form and fucking with it. This is narrative movie-making, which is what makes Pulp Video different from "underground" video or video art. Pulp Video IS cinema: "storytelling in words, music and pictures." But it should go further, shine light in areas that most narrative films avoid. This can be done through subject matter, or through unexpected honesty or vulnerability in characters, particularly "heroes." What Pulp Video isn't, is a place to practice making normal movies. Mind you, I'm sure there are other points of view. A class called Pulp Video has been flourishing at the San Francisco Art Institute for a few years now. Based on my manifesto, it bowdlerized the references to "exploitation," "violence" and "depravity," and spoke of Pulp Video as "The New Cinema." I haven't seen any of the results of this approach, which at first glance seems a bit more expansive than my definition. But it's important to realize that there's no point in making a movie in video that you could have made in film - unless you're creating a calling card to get you work in Hollywood. Pulp Video is about freedom; it's not about getting fitted for a pair of expensive shackles.

JS: Because of the cheap nature of the medium do you find you shoot too much footage?

CP: Yes. Particularly when I'm acting in a scene. That's why - whatever my next film or project may be - I don't want to be in it, even if it's just a cameo, because I will be in Hell for the ten minutes I'm on screen. I mean, the Spirit Drive cuts together fine, okay... but it was agony shooting it, because I was not able to

Rick Hall, Richard Kern in *Red Spirit Lake*

watch through the camera to see how things were framed. Watching the footage afterwards, there were places that I would have said, "Can you guys scoot over six inches?" As a result, **We Await** has some shots that literally took twenty takes, because I'm in them. And I'm the worst in terms of continuity because I don't do the same thing twice, so when I'm editing I just sit there hating myself. The other actors really did a great job, repeating movements take after take, doing what you are supposed to do to make it easier in the editing process. Meanwhile, my head would be turning a different way each time. I was terribly distracted. I was never sure if I was getting what I needed. Especially in the shots where no one was behind the camera. I'd set up the shot, press record, and then run into place. "Action!" It was crazy.

JS: Do you like acting?

CP: I don't know. I guess I do. I did it in high school, a little bit in college. I've done Shakespeare, Christopher Fry, Neil Simon. In high school everyone assumed I was going off to college to act. But I really don't think I'm prepared to plumb the necessary depths to be an actor. I would love to find some sort of niche playing baddies or sickos. I can play them fairly easily. I don't want to play sensitive guys with, like, problems and stuff. I already am that, I'm not interested in exposing myself that way. Well, I would, for the right director. [Jon] Moritsugu[8] for example, if he wanted me to do some whiny role, I'd do it; him, I would trust with that, because basically I think he's great.

JS: What about your short movie **Madball**, that stands out from your other work because it's shot on film.

CP: **Madball** was my first film, within three months of coming to Manhattan. I took a course at Film/Video Arts, there were five of us in the class, which ran six weeks, and we took turns being the crew in each other's work. Sort of the usual film class set-up. We were each given 400 ft of film. **Madball** is part of a trilogy about this character named Feller. There are actually two other chapters, also in black and white 16mm, which I haven't shot. I've never done anything as an exercise, it always seems to be part of what I'm trying to do, in a larger sense. With **Madball** I was the only person in the class who was like "This is my film"... Everybody else was learning. Well, I'm always learning... It's the same thing, when I was learning to play bass guitar, I formed Terence O'Doyle, and we began gigging immediately. I practice in public. I don't think everybody should, and I certainly don't want to watch other people practice in public. I'm sure some of the people who've suffered through my work feel the same way.

JS: Lets talk about **We Await**...

CP: **Madball**, **Killbillies**, Screw magazine... I was watching my years tick by in New York, which only totalled four, but it seemed at least two of those years were spent trying to get **Killbillies** made, and I just wanted to make a movie! So we made **Red Spirit Lake**, then moved out to San Francisco. We were going to start **Thousand Eyes** next - although at that point I only had a rudimentary idea about what **Thousand Eyes** was about. Again, it was Ellen's suggestion. She said "Look, you've already got the script for **Killbillies**, why don't we just make that?" So we decided to do **Killbillies**. We knew somebody who had a farm in Novato. **Killbillies** was like **The Texas**

Chainsaw Massacre – set in a totally remote area. "Terror has Some strange Kinfolk." Yee-hah! Then, one night, I went to a Hawkwind concert, and my perspective on the movie changed. Ironically, in the context of Pulp Video, Genesis was performing with Hawkwind at this concert. Anyway, at concerts, I usually just sort of space out; I don't necessarily even pay attention to the bands. It depends. What happened at this concert is that there was all this smoke, these lights, this mad music, and it just hit me: *We Await*. *Killbillies* distilled to its absolute viral essence. Take whatever smudge is left on the petri dish, and set the story in the Mission District in San Francisco, where we lived.

JS: Availablism again.

And the thing is, way back in New York, when I was trying to raise money for *Killbillies*, I always had the most fluid notion of where the movie could be set. Why not the warehouse district in Brooklyn? It didn't have to be in the country. The story is about these weird family dynamics. The essence of *Killbillies* didn't change by moving it to the Mission. You know, budget things changed, the scale of the story changed. We didn't crucify Tipple. We took a smaller, subtler approach. *We Await* is 54 minutes long, distilled from a two-hour movie. The interesting problem about adapting something, truncating something, is that you can still sometimes feel the phantom limbs. There are echoes of *Killbillies* in *We Await*, things that don't really make sense anymore... it's fine, because nobody notices them, but I look at them and say, "That's totally from *Killbillies*, it has nothing to do with *We Await*." Originally, the character I played, Barrett, had this cross bow and would wait by the side of this country road, and shoot people's tires out as they drove by. Then he'd kill them, take their cars, their clothes, their possessions. "Cannibalize "them, in more ways than one. Barrett had a car lot in the woods, filled with all these cars in varying degrees of decay. In his room was this wall of televisions, a dozen tvs, each tuned to a different station. The idea was that the members of the family were hyper-bright, they were just taking in all this information They were evolving rapidly, because they were hosts for the telepathic intelligence within the nectar. I don't know if you get a sense of that [in *We*

Production stills from *We Await*

Await]. There was just [in *Killbillies*] a real point made about their intelligence. Also, the family's patriarch had more of an overt shamanic experience in *Killbillies*, when he first discovers the crystal. And in *We Await*, all that's left of that is the line, "Knowledge tore me to pieces." I like *We Await* because I think in a way it is a little creepier. People see it and say "Is that back yard... that looks like a friend's back yard." It's just the Mission – all the back yards look like that. The idea was that this creepy family could be living right next door to you, not safely hidden in America's outback. They could be right next door. About a year after completing *We Await*, I walked into Tattoo City and everybody in there looked just like Barret: short hair, little goatee... It was pretty hilarious. Sean Heskett, from the band Phoenix Thunderstone, said of *We Await*, that you can't be too hip, cool or tattooed for this family, it really won't save you.

JS: *The Spirit Drive scene in* **We Await** *is pretty wild, and you also have been known to screen it separately, how did it come about?*

CP: You know, it goes back to *Killbillies*, and the genesis of that was George Cavano, a friend of mine in Gainesville. He used to come into this record store where I worked. He had possibly the most eclectic taste in Gainesville, always special ordering weird shit. Instead of a Spirit Walk, the family would take a Spirit Drive. The family take mushrooms or some other psychedelic, then walk to this car that's sitting on blocks – a total white trash thing – and then, in a double exposure, the Spirit Car drives off, leaving the actual car on blocks, and the family's corporeal forms sitting in the car. That was essentially

 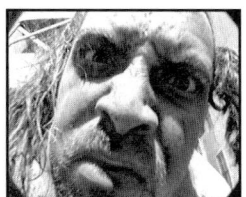 

Production stills from **We Await**

it. It was later, when working on the screenplay with John Walsh – another Screw staffer - that we came up with the events of the Spirit Drive. "Then they see Jesus. Yeah, that's good." I think it was Ellen who said "How about Dave Aaron Clark?" to play Jesus. And obviously he is great. The thing is that he didn't need much make up, the cuts and scar tissue are all there from his own performance work, so the only actual make-up on him was the third-eye wound on his forehead, and his monster teeth, and of course a lot of Karo syrup. Fake blood. That poor guy. It took us twelve hours or something, shooting against the blue screen.

*JS: How much did it cost to make **We Await** and **Red Spirit Lake**?*

CP: You know, I always say $2000. But I'm really pulling that figure out of a hat. It doesn't really cost anything to shoot on video. You do need to feed your cast and crew. That's essential.

JS: Do you do an off-line edit then an on-line edit?

CP: Never purely on-line, it's never time coded. Nothing was automated.
JS: A rough edit and then a master edit?

CP: Yeah. A rough edit, then a trim of that edit, followed by the laborious process of matching up the original tapes with the rough edit.

*JS: After you had completed **We Await** you then wrote the script for **Thousand***

Eyes again?

CP: The script for ***Thousand Eyes*** was never fully written or even rudimentary structured. Back in New York, I had a notion of what ***Thousand Eyes*** was about. Then, when I moved to the Bay Area I worked with autistic adults. One specific autistic adult I worked with became the basis for Jerry in ***Thousand Eyes***. Although Jerry is much more high functioning than the real-life guy; the real-life autistic guy couldn't pull off murdering people, cutting out their eyes, etc., much less hide the fact effectively. You know, Jerry's agenda, cutting out people's eyes and stuff, that's what Hitchcock would call a McGuffin. It's a spine upon which to pile all this other flesh. ***Thousand Eyes***, as the story exists now, comes out of the break-up with my wife. It's really about hubris, betrayal, and loss. And it basically wrote itself. As a tapestry, it's one kind of picture. But if you unravelled it and re-assembled its elements, the story would be about me. I'm all through the story. At times, during the writing, I would be surprised by where the story was going. At times I could tell that something vile was about to happen and I would be like, "My god!" I'd just observe the scene as it unfolded. The narrative was telling itself. There's a point in the script when the call-girl, Marty, is talking to the crime boss, Frostfree, and she says, "You know that book I was telling you about, The Breakdown Of Consciousness In The Bicameral Mind?" Marty spoke that line, I transcribed it, and then I stared slack-jawed at the screen. It was like, "I didn't know I was going to write that." The book she's referring to, by Julian Jaynes, deals with hearing voices. Did early man's notion of God come from voices leaking into the left lobe of his brain from the right lobe? I felt like, "My God, that's exactly what's happening to me right now: these other voices are talking to me, helping me write this script." It's an assessment that's hard to defend rationally, but I stand by it.

JS; How did you hook up with these guys in Hollywood?

CP: I was down in LA, screening ***We Await*** at the Hollywood SubCinema Night. A friend of mine edits in LA.

JS: Who, Tyler Hubby?

CP: Yeah, Tyler Hubby. Tyler introduces me to this guy, shows him **We Await**'s tape box, and said, "Charles made this movie". The guy says, "Can I look at it?" I was like, "Will I get it back?" I didn't know who he was. "Yeah you'll get it back." The guy leaves, and Tyler says "He distributes direct-to-video overseas." Weeks later I got a phone call from him and he said "Maybe we'd like to make a movie with you. Send me what you've got." So I sent him **Red Spirit Lake** and the script for **Thousand Eyes**. He got back to me, saying what he really wanted was for me to re-make **Red Spirit Lake**. So I spent maybe half a day trying to rework **Red Spirit Lake**, and it became **On Golden Pond**. Matthias became a very sympathetic character. Basically he was trying to redeem himself for his awful behavior in the first movie.

JS: He was given the power, the light, from the angels?

CP: Yeah, I guess. He and Marilyn enter some sort of Heaven place where they can make everything right. A second chance all around. Then Matthias and Marilyn would team up, kick some ass... And I thought, "No, I don't want to do this." Now it looks like they want to do **Thousand Eyes**, which would be great, since I want to do that movie, anyway. They used to work for Roger Corman, which is aces in my book.

JS: If they drop the project will you shoot it yourself?

CP: Absolutely. It really is a story I want to tell. As a purging of emotional and psychic garbage, just writing the script served its purpose. In that sense I'm finished with **Thousand Eyes**. But I'd also like to make the movie, as well.

*JS: What about this other project you started writing, **Dimension Door**?*

CP: That was originally conceived right after **Twisted Issues**. It's an incredibly involved narrative. David Aaron Clarke said, "Charles, this is a science fiction novel." Later he amended his statement to "a series of science fiction novels." So I'll admit it's kind of unworkable.

JS: *Didn't he later also say it should be a television mini-series?*

CP: I considered making it as a nine part series, shot on video, with each part being one hour...

JS: *Like Lars Von Trier's* **The Kingdom***?? Which is truly great, about five actors in the whole thing, really low budget, all shot on video...*

CP: Right, I love **The Kingdom**. On the level that I distribute my work, though, I don't know ... How would it be practical to distribute a nine hour video? It would have to enter some incredible cultdom for people to sit through it, it would have to be really fucking good.

JS: *It worked for Lars Von Trier.*

CP: The alternative is to distill this multivolume science fiction story into a movie. But there's so much detail in it. So many stories, characters, dimensions. At one point I thought, "It'll be an interactive CD-ROM." Now I just don't know. Maybe a comic book. Medium is less important to me than story. For this reason, I don't feel like a filmmaker. I'm a story-teller. I feel a deeper kinship to Flannery O'Connor than to Orson Welles.

¹ The horror films *Last House On The Left* (1972) and *The Hills Have Eyes* (1977) were both written and directed by Wes Craven, these films – like Pinion's – are characterized in part by their extreme violence and representation of humanity at its worst, similarly Pinion and Craven's films share the desire to use the trash/ gore of the exploitation genre yet simultaneously engage with mythic themes.

² Herschell Gordon Lewis directed the no budget Grand Guignol trio of sixties drive-in exploitation: *The Blood Feast* (1963), *2000 Maniacs* (1964), and *Color Me Blood Red* (1965), three films characterized by an incredible - even by today's standards - blood lust, and a willingness to luxuriate in the presentation of ultra-violence as a recognized visual pleasure. In addition to these acknowledged classics, Lewis also directed such cult hits as *A Taste Of Blood* (1967), *She Devils On Wheels* (1968), *Gruesome Twosome* (1968), *The Wizard Of Gore* (1970), and *The Gore Gore Girls* (aka *Blood Orgy*, 1972), as well as the nudie movies *The Prime Time* (directed under the name Gordon Weisenborn, 1960), *How To Make A Doll* (1968).

³ Ray Dennis Steckler directed some of the most legendary "incredibly strange films" (Jim Morton) ever to be projected including *Wild Guitar* (1962), *The Lemon Grove Kids Meet The Monsters* (1966), *Rat Pfink Boo Boo* (1966), and his undisputed masterpiece of the bizarre *The Incredibly Strange Creatures Who Stopped Living And Became Crazy Mixed-Up Zombie*s (1964). Steckler's movies are characterized via their willful neglect of the conventional standards of filmmaking and a gleeful disregard for the constraints of genre, style, or convention.

⁴ Directed by Peter Duffell, *The House That Dripped Blood* (1971) consists of four short stories by Robert Bloch, each of which is broadly concerned with the relationship between mimesis and magic.

⁵ The Russian film director Andrei Tarkovsky directed *Andrei Rublev* (1966, banned in Russia until 1971), *Solaris* (1972), *The Mirror* (1975), *Stalker* (1979), *Nostalgia* (1983), *The Sacrifice* (1986), these films were characterised by their slow pace and lyrical sense of visual beauty.

⁶ Chantel Akerman is director of *L'Enfant Aime* (1971), *News From Home* (1976), *The Eighties* (1983), and *From The East* (1993) amongst others, her films are characterised by an interest in human emotion rather than plots, which remain vague and non-specific in her work.

⁷ Roman Polanski has directed: *Knife In The Water* (1962), *Repulsion* (1964), *Rosemary's Baby* (1968), *Macbeth* (1971), *Chinatown* (1974), *The Tenant* (1976), *Tess* (1980) and *Frantic* (1988), amongst others. Polanski's films are largely concerned with protagonists who are alienated from their surroundings, occasionally to the point of insanity (as in *The Tenant*, *Macbeth*, and *Repulsion*), influenced by Alfred Hitchcock and Bunel, as well as writers such as Kafka and Beckett, Polanski's world is best characterized as uncanny.

⁸ Jon Moritsugu is the kick boy punk rock genius of the eighties underground, emerging simultaneously to the Cinema Of Transgression scene in Downtown New York, Moritsugu's films reveal similar concerns and interests, but luxuriate in a crazed style that is almost totally unique. Moritsugu mixes together found footage, original footage, and blasts of text-as-film in order to circumnavigate the dullness of conventional filmmaking. His films include *Terminal USA*, *My Degeneration*, and *Fame Whore* (1997).

9 Shot on video, Lars Von Trier's **The Kingdom** was broadcast as a television show, before being compiled for cinematic release. Set in a cursed hospital, the programme juxtaposes television genres in a disturbing mixture of comedy, horror, and soap opera.

Charles Pinion, San Francisco, 1997
Photo by Julie Peasley

Documenting The Underground

In recent years the role of the documentary film has increasingly emerged as one of the most important areas of independent cinema, functioning as both a means of disseminating information on the underground and, simultaneously, as a manifestation of underground culture[1]. Two recent video releases which, while almost antithetical in their approach, offer alternative views on the state of the underground are Chicago filmmaker Mark Hejnar's award winning[2] ultra-low budget *Affliction* and Blunt Cut's (the tag team of Julian Weaver and Mark Waugh) *Die Lieber Rausch (#1)*.

Hejnar's *Affliction* makes no secret of its desires to "appeal to the prurient interest" and offer "a prescription strength dose of mayhem for today's jaded voyeuristic audience". Shot (on a combination of video, a Fisher Price pixel camera, 8mm, super 8, and 16mm film) and collated from contributors videos over five years *Affliction* draws on a variety of wildly differing underground activists, artists and performers, including banned-from-drawing cartoonist Mike Diana, GG Allin, spree-killer in waiting Full Force Frank, genital-pierced/S&M band God Loves Over Dose, Annie Sprinkle (Post Porn Modernist show), Kembra Pfahler's band The Voluptuous Horror of Karen Black, etc. Hejnar states, "I didn't begin the project with a list of people or anything like that. There were a few core performers I was working with, and I added others as the idea evolved over time to the finished document. ...The performers involved don't really form a 'scene', although some do work together. They compliment each other"[3].

The material on *Affliction* is frequently extreme, often hilarious, and occasionally nauseating. An old friend of GG's, Hejnar has included footage of the fecal-rock ubermensch at his filthy peak: firstly filmed squirting shit over his audience, then turning in a great performance backstage. Here GG utilizes a groupie's rectum as a post-enema dispenser for tomato ketchup (which drizzles from her ass in a most unsatisfactory manner) and beer (which sprays a glorious brown and yellow shower over GG's face and torso. Another highlight of *Affliction* is the footage of Mike Diana, which was filmed by Diana in his bedroom at his father's house and then sent to Hejnar. Diana – aided by his then girlfriend Suzy 'Morbid' Smith – supplies a great/absurd voice over to his strip 'The Dinner Date'. Additional sequences depict Diana

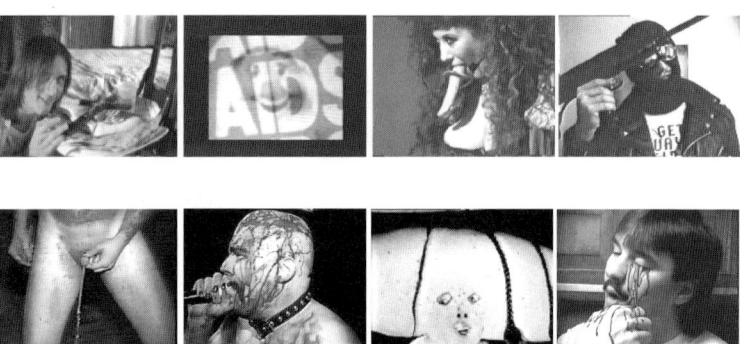

Affliction stills - clockwise from top left: Mike Diana about to vomit on a cross, AIDS yet, Annie Sprinkle, Full Force Frank, Turbo Tom with a skewer through his face, Becky, G.G. Allin, G.G. Allin pissing

taking an emetic ("epicaptor syrup" he informs the camera) and violently vomiting over a Bible and crucifix. Later he holds the crucifix next to his hard-penis, and states "my cock is the same size as Jesus on the cross.... That's what God is... a fucking dick", finally he masturbates stroking his erection, with the crucifix jammed into his rectum.

Some of the most extreme footage used in **Affliction** is that of Turbo Tom. Filmed on location in Lowell, at the University Of Massachusetts, in front of an audience of shocked teens, Turbo Tom is a "one man freak show". Tom uses his back for a dart board, has his face pierced with a skewer, sticks a pair of scissors into the space between his eyelid and eye, and snaps his hand in a massive animal trap: "Don't try this at home".

But, by far the most 'disturbing' footage, is that of For Love, a video sent in by Joel Bender, Hejnar: "An article in Obscure Publications about **Affliction** mentioned I was still seeking submissions. He was the only one who responded, and what a fucking response!" The footage – shot in close up – features a male masturbating into a friend's face, as he ejaculates he sticks a pin into the head of his erect penis. Blood squirts out, onto the other man's face. The camera does not move as the blood continues to squirt out, arching in a stream with every pulse, spraying red globs of bloody cum over the man's cheek, nose, forehead, lips, and eyes. The footage seems to go on for a long time. Hejnar rarely mentions this piece, which closes **Affliction**, because he "saves the best for last and [does] not [want to] disappoint the audience".

The emphasis on the 'shocking' which is frequently manifested through sex and violence, and Hejnar's recognition of the audience's salacious scopophilia, position the film not just as an underground documentary, but also as the logical heir to that most salacious of genres: the Mondo Movie, which stylistically is equal parts freak show, anthropology, and Circus Maximus. Hejnar recognizes the audience's collective desire for shock, and, at one point, literally signposts it via a subtitle which introduces the GG Allin section as "The bit you've been waiting for".

Die Lieber Rausch (#1) is directed, edited and compiled by the English production company, Blunt Cut, and as such engages with a different history of the underground (not least because of the involvement of the Arts Council in funding this film, suggesting a far different engagement with the dissemination of 'culture' than America)[4]. ***Die Lieber Rausch*** was/is a nightclub/performance arena which ran in Brighton in Spring 1995 and 1996. Each event featured music, film, and performance which was either premiering or specially commissioned for the evening[5]. The artists showcased were filmed simultaneously on 16mm, super 8, 8mm, and video, resulting in a radical stylistic mix which cuts between materials regardless of any totalising artistic tradition. This film is the first of a proposed series of videos depicting the most interesting work at the cutting edge of the performance world, among

Affliction movie poster

YX and *Hong Kong Phooey*

the artists included on this first video release are; Breadman Tatsumi Orimoto, Bhuto performer Masaki Iwana, 'cyber' performer/body explorer Bruce Gilchrist, the burlesque music hall singer and dancer of Marisa Carr, in addition to the Gulf War/amphetamine rants of Adrian Challis, and the static beauty of Drako. Like the artists on Affliction these performers have little in common, sharing only a desire to push their own creative boundaries.

Stylistically **Die Lieber Rausch** emphasizes its own construction, repeatedly using funky looking computer graphics and manipulations to emphasize and punctuate the artists work. Thus, for example, super 8 loop footage of Marisa Carr (in her incarnation as the Dragon Lady) is manipulated to form a dancing frame around her face during an interview, Bruce Gilchrist's work is introduced via computerized text flashing across the screen, and Tatsumi Orimoto's slow psychogeographical explorations (undertaken while his face is smothered in loaves of bread) are presented speeded up, increasing the emphasis on his otherness by separating his near stationary body from the clumsy crowds around him.

Although more apparently engaged with (and perhaps beholden to) the aesthetic and philosophical questions in contemporary art than **Affliction**, **Die Lieber Rausch** – while sharing few of the prurient thrills – is, at times, as visceral. One of the video's high points is its depiction of Bruce Gilchrist's Divided Resistance performance, during which Gilchrist

Drako

was tattooed with a large reproduction of his thumb print on his shoulder (filmed in close up), while electrodes on his body amplified his biological and electrochemical responses to the pain of the needle. The resulting soundtrack is an excruciatingly loud combination of dissonant whistles, hums, throbs, and squeaks, reminiscent of the extreme manifestations of noise music. While this transpires, an audience member wears a bullet proof vest covered in electronic circuitry, which enables her/him to feel Gilchrist's body's responses to the process of receiving a tattoo.

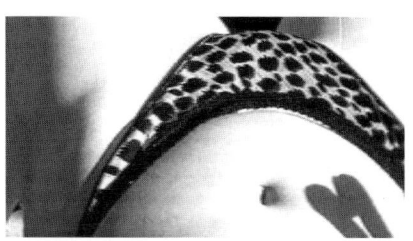
above: Marisa's gut
below: *Internal*

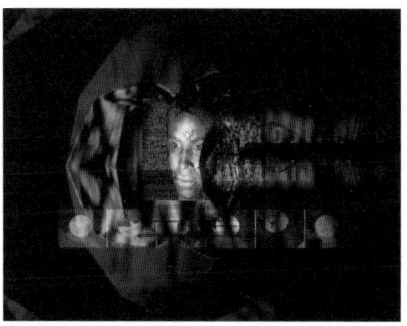

An equally powerful moment emerges in the hypnogogic stillness of Drako's performance Bliss: A Body Modification. Best known as an actor in Jarman's *The Garden*, Drako's performance consists of standing naked on stage and very slowly turning around, revealing his beautiful body tattoos, and his pierced and decorated genitals. *Die Lieber Rausch (#1)* is a catalogue of the genuinely interesting in performance art, and the second edition, rumored to be in pre-production, should hopefully be available soon.

What the artists documented and the producers of both *Affliction* and *Die Lieber Rausch* share is a belief in disseminating radically heterogeneous world views. Both videos offer brief views into other worlds, and other possibilities, yet neither video is evangelical. Both films recognize that speed is of the essence, and nothing on either release lasts longer than is absolutely necessary. Most important of all, these two films are a testament to the importance of the underground documentary in all of its manifestations.

[1] The most famous, and 'well produced' of these new documentaries are Todd Phillips' legendary GG Allin flick *Hated: GG Allin And The Murder Junkies*, and Adi Sideman's infamous NAMBLA documentary *Chickenhawk – Men Who Love Boys*.

[2] Hejnar's movie was awarded Best Documentary at the 1996 Chicago Underground Film Festival, for the first time in the festival's three year history the juries decision was unanimous.

[3] All quotes attributed to Mark Hejnar are from personal correspondence.

[4] Indeed it is perhaps incorrect to refer to most of these performers as 'underground', it is perhaps only Marisa Carr and Drako who can genuinely be said to be, or to have been, involved with the 'underground'. The rest of the performers here are better described as avant garde.

[5] One coup being a screening of Jarman's *Journey To Avebury* with a new soundtrack by Coil.

True Stories About True Gore

The World of Monte Cazazza

"Why do we watch a car accident on the freeway, or rush to see a fire – to drink in the tempestuous loveliness of terror, or simply to catch a glimpse of our destiny?" – True Gore

"That's my primary goal. To get on people's nerves. So I always try and have something in them which I'm sure will get on somebody's nerves. And it's not a success unless people...or somebody...walks out, as far as I am concerned" – Monte Cazazza.

Opening with the credit "The Gore Brothers Present..." True Gore (1986) is the logical heir to the mondo movie, that bizarre genre that welds together the freak show, anthropological curiosity, and pure, salacious voyeurism. Directed by Matthew Causey, with Monte Cazazza credited as "creative consultant", the low-budget True Gore is reminiscent of the later, more notorious, mondo movies such as **Faces Of Death** (Conan Le Cilaire, 1979), and its many sequels. While these now-legendary genre films were produced for box office release most were considered too extreme, even for the sleazoid crowds inhabiting the scummy cinemas of 42nd Street and Times Square, and it was on video that they found their audience. In recognition of this **True Gore**, like many of the mondo movies of the late eighties, was produced directly on video.[1]
Divided into four sections – **The World Of The Dead, The Eroticism Of Decay, Art And Death**, and **The Science Of Death** – **True Gore** feigns an attempt at structural coherence, but the optical effects created using a video synthesizer and designed to mask the identity of the film's unnamed narrator, the purposefully clichéd narration, and the occasionally misspelled subtitles, belie its low budget. However, this should not be used as a reason to decry the film, so much as it should be seen as a signifier to other mondo texts, which themselves are in part characterized by their less than pristine appearance, indeed the style adds to the illicit thrills offered by the genre. Like many of the later mondo films, **True Gore** focuses primarily on images of injury, death and decay[2], however, in addition to those images familiar to the genre, the film also contains many segments culled from Monte Cazazza's

True Gore videobox

own underground filmmaking practice[3].

The first section of the film – **The World Of The Dead** – consists of re-photographed images collected from medical textbooks and police training manuals, forensic pathology and medical education films, and some original footage shot in a morgue. These grisly images of damaged and rotting flesh are followed with clearly faked footage of a suicide victim laying in a blood filled bathtub, casually slashed wrist dangling over the side of the bath, blood dripping onto the linoleum floor[4]. Where this section becomes most disturbing is in its usage of the aural footage of Jim Jones' last speech as 956 members of the People's Temple commit suicide slurping cyanide contaminated fruit juice. The suicide soundtrack – dubbed over photographs depicting various iconographic elements of the People's Temple, including their discipline room – was taken from Cazazza's extensive archive, and was also released as a picture disc by the World Satanic Network Service[5].

As the film's second section starts the narrator states, with a showman's faux cynicism, "in the underground of the world these films are created for the sickest minds". This is followed by a collage of shots taken from the legendary First Transmission video depicting scenes of ritualized SM sexual experimentation. These images are familiar to anybody who witnessed Psychic TV in their pre-acid house daze. Cazazza was, of course, a regular collaborator with P. Orridge and Psychic TV. The accompanying extra-diagetic soundtrack consists of Cazazza's 'Sex Is No Emergency'. This segment also contains images −"from Amnesty International" the narrator states − depicting a man being suspended over an oil-drum filled with water, before being dunked and beaten. For added effect a snake is thrown over the drowning man's head. The footage is fake. The victim is Cazazza. This scene is followed by some genuinely disturbing images of vivisection: a live pig is tied down and military scientists stand over it holding a blow-torch, which is then played slowly across the squealing animal's flesh which rapidly blackens, burns, and splits open. Next a cat has its scalp pealed and a chunk of its brain removed, as the narrator observes, such experiments appear as senseless exercises. These images of genuine cruelty appear all the more horrific because of their juxtaposition with the fake footage.

True Gore's third section, **Art And Death**, focuses once more on Cazazza's underground movies, as the narrator wryly comments, "at least it was self inflicted" the sequence is edited from Cazazza's 13 minute Super 8

Monte Cazazza and friends, 1997
Photo by Julie Peasley

collaboration with Tana Emmolo Smith, *SXXX-80* (1980), a film which gleefully depicts what many would consider polymorphic sexual dysfunction as home movie, and was produced as a result of equal parts ennui and mischief on Cazazza's part. The extract presented in *True Gore* depicts Cazazza digging at a sore on his penis with a metal scalpel, and Smith letting a gigantic black centipede scuttle over her labia. Mimicking the fake-decorum of the death film genre, Smith's vagina and Cazazza's penis, both of which are visible in the original short film, are hidden behind tastefully positioned black squares, this is after all not a sex film.[6]

The extract from *SXXX-80* is followed by a sequence taken from the 40 minute video *Night Of The Succubus* (1981) which documents a chaotic performance between Cazazza, Survival Research Laboratories and San Francisco post-industrial band Factrix. From this ostensibly performance art documentation the film returns to the theme of necrophilia and lustmord. The ensuing footage, supposedly depicting two psychotic paraphyliacs, is faked, with a female necrophile played by artist Debra Valentine, and a male murderer played by Cole, who, despite being in shade, should be familiar to the film's audience, having just appeared in the previous scene playing guitar and singing with Factrix. The performances given by these actors are convincing primarily because the scenes were shot in one take, with the actors

Monte Cazazza, 1997
Photo by Julie Peasley

reading from a script, the occasional stumbled words and phrases serving to create a haunting, confessional atmosphere.

The film introduces the thematic of AIDS as the latest plague threatening to annihilate humanity. Notably, given the media treatment of the virus as "gay" and "junkie plague" at the time of *True Gore*'s production, the film draws attention to the fact that AIDS is a disease that can attack anyone "we are all victims", drawls the narrator. Genuine autopsy footage ends the section of the film.

The Science Of Death – *True Gore*'s final section – consists primarily of stock footage depicting the shivering survivors of the Nazi Death Camps, which is intercut with images from Leni Riefenstahl's *Triumph Of The Will* (1934). This is followed by what the narrator describes as "our homage to the Scientific Age": To the Atom Smashers' song 'A Is For Atom' the film juxtaposes images from Cold War propaganda films, scientific cartoons explaining radiation, and images of the burned and mutilated survivors of Nagasaki and Hiroshima.

The film closes with the narrator walking through a graveyard telling the audience "to live in fear of death is a waste of life". A short, sombre scene follows, depicting row-upon row of tombstones. The soundtrack consists of church bells. The camera spins through the graveyard and positions the viewer gazing out from an open grave. This cuts to the image of a laughing mechanical clown, once more suggesting the carney roots of the mondo genre, and the wound black humour of *True Gore*'s aesthetic.

✶

[1] Other direct to video mondo film's include Nick Bougas' excellent *Death Scenes* (1989) and *Death Scenes 2* (1992), and the Brain Damage production *Traces Of Death* (1993).

[2] Earlier mondo movies – produced in the sixties – whilst presenting some violent images, also luxuriated in scenes of indigenous cultures (and especially those cultures for whom nudity is a norm), nudist colonies, occult ceremonies, and safari scenes, all of which have subsequently become visual staples on television. The genre's interest in sex and sexuality boomed in the early seventies, with titles such as Alex De Rezny's *Sexual Encounter Group* (1970), *Sex And Astrology* (1970), and *Sexual Freedom In Denmark* (1970), as well as Pat Rocco's *Sex And The Single Gay* (1970), but was rapidly rendered as pointless with the explosion and subsequent availability hardcore

pornography in the seventies (following the massive success of Gerard Damiano's **Deep Throat** which – in 1972 – served to partially legitimize hardcore, and also served to show the massive market for such movies). Finally it was the continued taboos surrounding violence and death that remained, and these have subsequently become the focal point of mondo movies. This thematic eruption is also due to the increasing availability of footage depicting violence and death, due – primarily – to the popularity of video technologies which are utilized by news gathering teams, as well as the emergency services, thus guaranteeing a virtual glut of available visceral footage.

3 Cazazza has directed, produced, and collaborated on a string of movies, including, amongst others: **Revolt 2000** (1974) in which he acts like a terrorist and builds a bomb using information from *Assassin* magazine, the film is now lost. **Diary Of A Rubber Slave** (1976) subsequently stolen, **Mondo Homo** (1976) – another engagement with the mondo genre, filmed in secret at the notorious gay bar The Slot, the film was one of the first to depict fist fucking – subsequently stolen. **Mystery Movie** (co-directed with Genesis P. Orridge, 1976, whereabouts unknown). **Death Wish** (1977), consisting of re-photographed TV footage. **Black Cat Tea** (co-directed with Mary Quayzar, 1979/80), **Behind The Iron Curtain** (1980), **SXXX-80** (co-directed with Tana Emmolo Smith, 1980), **Night Of The Succubus** (co-directed with Factrix, 1981), and **Catscan** (with Michelle Handelman, 1989). In addition Cazazza has produced and collaborated with Handelman on **Blood Sisters** (1991), and collaborated with Psychic TV on the videos **Terminus** and **Eden Three** (1987).

4 The usage of re-constructed/fake footage is one of the central aspects of the mondo genre in its latter incarnation as a grim sideshow of annihilation: "Although many of the sequences involving killings were fabricated, the filmmakers attempted to make distinguishing fake from fact as difficult as possible" (David Kerekes and David Slater, *Killing For Culture, An Illustrated History Of Death Film From Mondo To Snuff*, Creation Books, 1995 [first published 1994] p.113).

5 The World Satanic Network Service aka Vagina Dentata Organ released a string of records documenting various extreme events, including Cold Meat, which consisted of the sound of somebody breathing – and dying – whilst on an infribulator, and came as a picture disc depicting photographs of Maralyn Monroe and Elvis Presley in death.

6 It is an oddity of the mondo genre that, whilst depicting death with glee, depictions of sexual organs are less common, with producers and directors frequently choosing to hide them behind visual effects. This reaches its zenith in **Death Women** – a Japanese film of unspecified date and direction – which depicts extreme images of female corpses – strangled, crushed, torn, ripped, savaged, and burned - yet tastefully pixellates any images of the corpses' pubic region and vaginas.

Baby Blatzo Vs Dr. Gaz:

The Cinematic Visions of Mr. Soft Eliminator Jeff Keen

"It rubs the very noses of our mannequins in our own mold and sends us spinning into the street undone and toothless" – Jack Smith on Jeff Keen's *Autumn Feast*.

Jeff Keen's two room Brighton apartment is a crowded tangle of cardboard props, old Godzilla and Clint Eastwood posters, shelves crammed with leather bound books and thousands of comics and toys. Toys, or the remains of, litter every surface: tin robots, replica guns, pieces of Action Men, Sindy dolls, rubber super heroes and cheesy Rambo action figures, and packets of unopened *Made-In-Korea* toy soldiers purchased from the local fifty pence shop. In the kitchen there is even a small dish filled with some undoubtedly lethal toy explosives: 'Bomb Bags: just squeeze and throw: harmless: Made-In-China'. His films are stacked neatly in cupboards, or in special display boxes; **ARTWAR** sits in an old ammunition box with the title stencilled on the side. Old pieces of unedited film hang in convenient spaces; below shelves and inside cupboards. On one wall hangs a massive blank sheet of white paper, the current backdrop to Jeff's films, a cursory inspection reveals that behind the paper the wall is splashed and streaked with twenty-five years worth of paint and glue from previous productions.

Jeff Keen has been producing underground movies since 1960, making his career the longest in England, and because the American underground movies were unseen until '64, Keen felt that he was "working in a vacuum"[1]. His movies are a combination of visual collage, animation, and live action 'spectacle'. Frequently the films combine all three styles, reflecting Jeff's own experiences of cinema before the arrival of the soulless multiplex entertainment experience, when going to the movies meant viewing news reels, cartoons, a B movie, and the feature. By combing three styles into one movie Keen is attempting to create a condensed version of this experience. Inspired by B movies, the pre-War pulps he read as a teenager, fifties men's magazines (*Confidential*, *Man's Adventure*), and comics (*The Punisher* is a current favorite), Jeff's films are populated by characters with names such as Dr Gaz, Baby Blatzo, Silverhead, Mr Soft Eliminator, The Catwoman, and the Breathless Investigator.

Artwar promotional graphic, 1993

For the most part the films are incredibly fast paced. His most recent body of work **ARTWAR**, commissioned in part by Channel Four[2], was designed so that it could be shown as a whole, or cut up into thirty second fragments and 'dropped' in by the broadcasters (an idea inspired by modern advertising and the use of two adverts; a full and abbreviated version). As Jeff points out, the speed of the thirty-second fragments would leave the viewer sitting dumbfounded and asking themselves, "what the fuck was all that about?" Channel Four lacked Jeff's vision, and decided to broadcast the film as a 'cohesive' whole, rather than risk cutting it up.

A mine of information, able to articulate on subjects including philosophy, independent film production, the histories of notorious B movies, underground films, comic book characters, performance artists, guns, and the counter culture, Jeff was interviewed at home, over an afternoon tea of chocolate roll and crumpets. Also present was his daughter, performer, filmmaker and artist, Stella Starr.

Jack Sargeant: When did you start filmmaking?

Jeff Keen: Where, or when? Not here [gestures around the room] but not far away, at the Art College, not that I was directly connected with the Art College, more that I was drawn in, as it were. I helped found the Student's Film Society, just for showing films really, but then they acquired an 8mm camera and editing gear, and started making films. But since all the students – mostly graphics students – who were involved in the film society were so busy collecting work for their folders they didn't have time to make movies for the end of term show so I had to step in and make the films, hence films like ***The Time Is Now*** and ***Wail***, made during 1960 - 62.

JS: Was that animation or live action?

JK: Mixed. Both. So I had a go at a number of little movies, even made a little film noir as they say – Robin Blashky starred in ***Breakout*** – in which he wanders around the town trying to break into people's cars and homes unsuccessfully (laughs). Then goes to a midnight movie show at the Princes News Theatre. It's shot on quite fast Perutz film, made in East Germany, and Orwo film (laughs), it had a nice texture.

JS: At what point did you start shooting for yourself, rather than through the college?

JK: I continued with short animations, and then, during 64/65 I made a twin screen film [***The Pink Auto***], shot on the rubbish tip. Lots of improvised actions, found objects.

JS: What do you like about the rubbish tip, because you go and shoot up there all the time?

JK: I used to, but not anymore, it's now fenced off – forbidden territory.

Stella Star: It was great because all the props were already there.

JK: ...And I used to go and collect scraps, plastic toys, to build into collages.

SS: They used to have whole burnt out cars there.

JK: And loads of furniture, you could actually furnish a home out there, easily.

JS: What I find interesting, especially in regard to finding trash props – you seem to use things you find for props, you don't seem to make props, like the masks you've used which are masks you get from toy stores, not ones you've made. It's like "this is good. I'll use it", is this aesthetic a thing that has come from collage, the appropriation of an existing image rather than...

JK: Yes, right, yes. Also when you're making a collage – actually this applies to painting too doesn't it – you are making the thing up as you go along. You know, Picasso's thing about red and blue "if I haven't got blue I'll put red in" often quoted I know, but it is true. I mean if you're going in one direction and it doesn't work you pick up something and put that in the painting and off it goes in another direction. Of course that's not how commercial movies are made – they're usually made with tight scripts and are well planned beforehand. But if you are working on your own you can work on a principle much closer to collage in that you can add and subtract as you go. Right, you can, say, pick up a mask and that suggests something, in the way that characters can suggest certain roles... you've got to have a female lead, a male lead, and a villain. And, if you are lucky, you get a good monster to come on (laughs)....and you can make a movie that way. I'm sure the people who are making those really cheap horror videos[3] are basically working on that principle, they make them with what they can get hold of. That's what I have always done, yeah.

JS: And the same people again and again.

Jeff Keen

JK: That's right – The Family Star Players. John Ford[4] films were made with the same people over and over again, and they develop, that was the interesting thing: the characters develop over the movies.

JS: There is a development in your films, like the diary films, not just historically but stylistically, so you started shooting on one camera, one image, then two, then four so you have four images projected, so the way you show films has developed...

JK: Yes. That's right. The twin screen thing came quite naturally really. In **The Pink Auto** (a film for two projectors) a character would run off the screen and – with any luck – appear in the other one (laughs) and continue the action. They never really [do]... (laughs). Today, of course, [with] computer controlled images all sorts of things like that can happen.

JS: The chaos and spontaneity, where someone might walk from one screen to the next seems far more entertaining than computer stuff where you can time it all, because that just removes the chaos. When you show two films side by side it never comes out the same.

JK: It never comes out the same. You're right.

JS: So every time you screen it you're creating the whole thing again.

JK: Constant re-creation.

JS: That ties in with your performance, the performances around the films change, and develop[5].

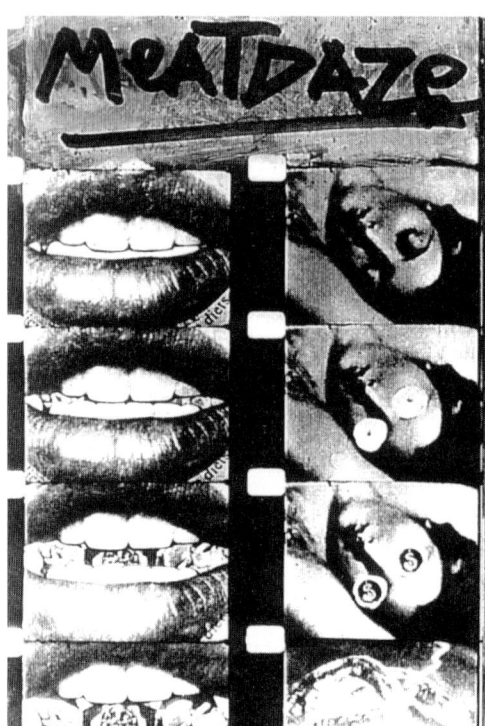

Jeff Keen, *Meatdaze*

JK: Yes, I think that little performance at the end there[6], was so different from other ones I'd done, whether that is because it was set up rather tightly with two camera men – which is a bit intimidating really – they were covering the action. And they were so worried about the sound being so rough, but it was the roughness I wanted really. [I] had an old guitar practice amp and the inevitable echo chamber, putting the sound through that was just what I wanted. But they wanted to work with a purer sound and mess it up afterwards for atmosphere.

JS: It's best to start with the sound screwed up already.

JK: I like that noise because it echoed all around the cave. They actually altered the whole building, they completely gutted it and remodeled it. But at that time it was a nice, damp, cold cavern. Actually, you know, we did shows there in the late sixties, of all things.

Jack: What kind of stuff was going on then?

JK: Poetry readings and films. And people used to do shows there – the audiences were all beachniks. Really crazy characters, they'd love everything [stoned voice] "wow!", no matter what really happened they'd love it (laughs). In '68 when we did this weekend performance which went into the film **Meatdaze**, the only sane people there were the mad people performing.

SS: What were they doing?

JK: Themes from French paintings, a little picnic on the grass, so there was a bit of nudity, lamps all around like a movie set up, big monster sandwiches and so on. Jim Duke with a hacksaw cutting up things and melting them and putting them in water. Madly improvised, well not that mad, it was controlled actually. A little controlled theatre piece. It was the audience that were mad (laughs).

SS: Were they all on acid?

JK: They were straight from sunbathing on the beach I think, their little brains were addled.

JS: That's interesting that you mention Jim sawing, because destruction seems to come into your films quite a lot.

JK: Absolutely. Yes.

JS: Like you have said in the past about cutting strips of films and editing them together randomly, according to chance, the Dada thing, or as in the **ARTWAR** *stuff, where you paint all these great pictures and then set fire to them and drag them down the road and stuff. So it's like a part of your art comes from things being destroyed. I was just wondering if you could say a bit about why...*

JK: Yes. I suppose destruction is part of the creative process really. The practical consideration with **ARTWAR** [is] getting rid of things (laughs) – what a way to go. Then I found God did it for me; I kept all my paintings in the greenhouse – no where else to keep them – and they were destroyed by mould, some of the patterns were quite artistic actually, little mould and snail [trail] patterns all over them (laughs). They just crumble into dust when I pick them up, I quickly took photographs – I've got a lot of them on slides before they completely fell apart. Then they had to go back to the tip, where I gathered most of the stuff, so it's a constant process of creation and destruction, but perhaps one shouldn't use 'creative'. Only a creator creates, isn't that right? Everything else is imitation, mimesis. We're all copy cats really.

JS: It strikes me as interesting that destruction is not just a visual spectacle of the movies but also a theme, war and stuff...

JK: Yes, you are right, of course. War is a monstrous version of that, isn't it, where armies are disciplined and shaped into a work of art marching into war. And then, when it happens of course, it is all totally irrational, like a disease or something unstoppable. Once a war starts it's unstoppable, until it burns itself out.

JS: The other thing I'm really interested in is the speed of your films. What was

comic by Jeff Keen

it you said about the human brain, that it works on 24...?

JK: 24 frames per second sound speed, 16 frames per second silent. Yes.

JS: But speed is really fascinating.

JK: When I first started getting animation to work – it was too slow I found. I was doing it in a clumsy sort of way you know, not really getting things to move, I suppose I spent most of the time really trying to find ways of relating still pictures to moving pictures. Sometimes by painting over a still picture so it merges into the next one, or burning things, so there is a movement from one still to another which creates an illusion of constant movement. But otherwise its cut, cut, cut which can become tiresome. I don't take it as far as Robert Breer, in some of his early things he made every frame a different shot[7]. But what I did with, say, **CineBlatz,** was just to take a page from a magazine and draw on it and flick through very quickly to the next, so you couldn't linger on the image. One finds that you can get by with two or three frames sometimes, you know, pack a lot into a fraction of a second. Working on cinema on a frame by frame basis you end up with short films (laughs) you don't make epics or long films. They are peripheral aren't they to the history of cinema, in a way – don't you think?

JS: Well, not to me.

JK: They are to most people – they think "oh, yeah they're little animated films" or whatever and they don't get in cinema's of course, but then, is that really necessary?

JS: I find it very interesting that a lot of the images in your films come from comics, what is it about comics that you like?

JK: It's the colour and the drawing that I like first of all, I think. I don't know if you've read Baudelaire's essays on art, he wrote a thing on toys, and

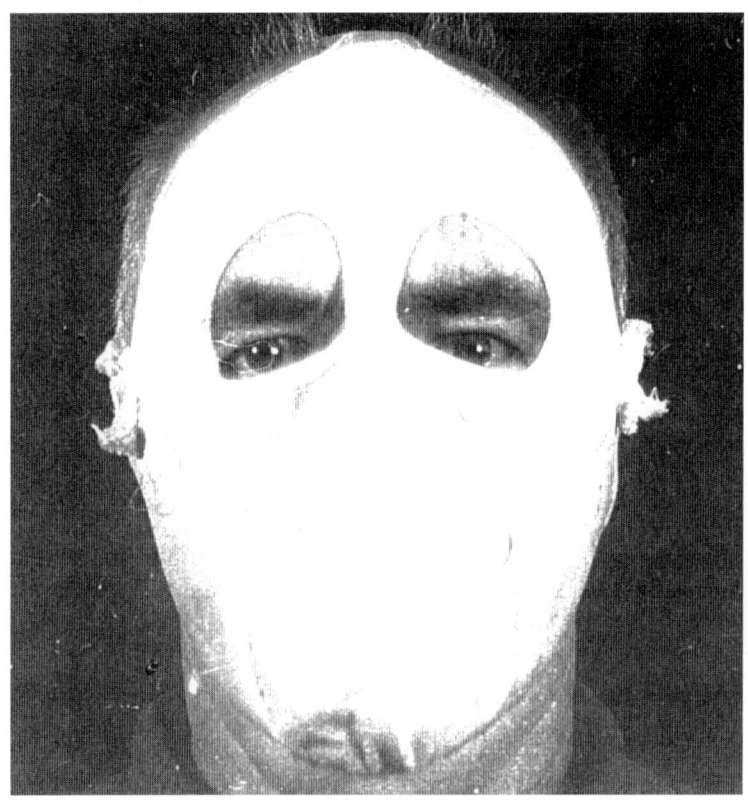

Dr.Gaz in *Gazwrx* (super 8)

children's attitudes to toys and so on? The fact that they were richly coloured and that children couldn't resist picking them up and playing. And I think that's the great thing about comics, they've gone more realistic now – more naturalistic perhaps – but originally they did have that kind of, not exactly primitive quality, but they were outside the world of bourgeoisie art.

JS: They had an aesthetic of their own, probably partly due to paying people low wages and printing them cheaply.

JK: That I like: the fact that they were printed so badly, the colours overlapping, it gave them a certain rawness. They were hermetic! That's what I was trying to think of. They obey a law to themselves – you get Doll Man and Plastic Man and you know they are going to act in a certain physical way. Plastic Man would burst from frame to frame and go through the story, a kind of driving force. Superman and Batman were like that too, in

Jeff Keen at work on **ARTWAR**

the early days, now they are psychologising all the time. Ever since Spiderman got all kind of neurotic they are questioning their motives and being too subjective, they are not acting according to instinct. Those early characters were creatures of instinct acting directly, as distinct from characters in novels who are always questioning their feelings. Now Batman does just that of course...

JS: *The colours from toys and comics is something I see in your films...*

JK: Well look at these toys! I feel it very difficult to resist them. I do resist buying them, [but] you see a wall of toys in Woolworth's, a great wall of toys...a lot of art goes into them.

JS: The colours in your paintings which you use in the films are like that, with all the lurid reds and blues...

JK: Yes. In a way I rather like video because you can soup up the colours sometimes. I know it's not done, people tend to frown on that. I went into the art college once to try something out and a teacher there said "we don't recommend to the students that they try all that", we try to restrain them, in other words, from playing with all the amazing colours.

JS: But it seems to me that, if you can get these colours, you should at least play with them.

JK: Absolutely, playing is the thing, yes.

JS: There seems to be a lot of play in your films. In the way you shoot them, screen them, and the images you are using. Maybe even humour.

JK: I find jokes difficult now. I don't do jokes anymore (laughs), the humour is

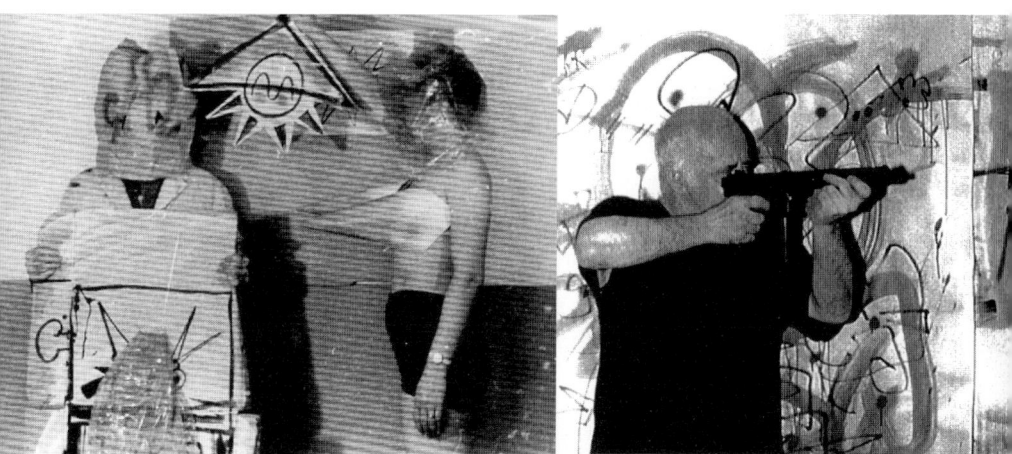

like childish humour, destructive, and of course some of these Hollywood action films have that quality, they exploit it sometimes, don't they, with the Arnie [Arnold Schwarzenegger] films, they give him a whole host of one liners to go with the violent actions he performs and take the edge off them.

JS: They seem a little forced to me. It's not like going to watch a film like a Chuck Norris[8] film and laughing at it, and now they try to put themselves across as intellectual.

JK: Sure, I agree that some of the later action films are like that. Too self regarding and too aware, like that recent Schwarzenneger movie....

JS: *True Lies*[9]?

JK: *True Lies* [which was] billed as a postmodern deconstructive thing. Once you start doing that you are on the way out.

JS: There is a way in which your films could be said to be postmodern though, for example with the loaf of bread with nails in it which resembles Surrealism..

JK: But then, of course, I grew up with that, I felt that I could play with it. The Surrealists were the first breakthrough for me really, because there was hardly any modern art in this country until the forties, for years only one Picasso was shown publicly anywhere in London, and that wasn't representative of his work. It was just kept out really. In fact we didn't have an exhibition of Cubism until 1947.

JS: Thirty years later.

JK: So really you couldn't see anything, and for me it was a revelation to go into a gallery and see something that was non-representational and quite free in its feelings. Not modern in the sense of being modernistic – but being free. Expressing freedom. And that was a terrific experience. It's hard to imagine what an artistic desert England was at that time.[There is] something a bit depressing about the English reaction [to art]. I think perhaps because we've been cut off we think things have got to be serious all the time in some way or another, to show they are fine art or serious art.

JS: It is the same with English cinema where all that is cited in text books, all that is praised, is early Ealing Studios films[10] and kitchen sink dramas, rather than Hammer movies[11] or Carry On films[12], all those huge things are ignored. It is as if there is an embarrassment about popular culture in England.

JK: Oh, definitely, yeah. It is the class thing to some extent I suppose. And also a feeling of cultural inadequacy.

JS: I always thought that it was a thematic of your **ARTWAR** stuff, declaring yourself against certain definitions of what is art?

JK: I have certainly taken an anti-art position, you know. It is all too precious and it is time to blow it away. But in that **ARTWAR** video I didn't really set out to be satirical in any way, or really adopt a critical attitude as such. I just like the idea of burning things (laughs) blowing up artworks (laughs).

JS: Okay, what about all these guns?

JK: The handgun is a beautiful machine. Of course it's deadly, destructive… a machine for destroying. But you can see why people are attracted to it, because it condenses power. It fits the hand beautifully. I always thought the handgun and the bike are the two most beautiful machines invented. The bike fits your bum and legs, the handgun fits – perfectly – the trigger finger. (laughs) And it gives that sense of power, it is like having a little motor there: action and reaction when it goes off [demonstrating shooting with an air pistol, and the kick of the gun]. It's like having a little engine. A destructive engine of course. But a beautiful machine. And it concentrates everything on that point. That is why I like the old fashioned cowboy films which end with the shoot-out. There is that tension isn't there [in cowboy voice] "pull it too fast or too slow..." it's just a test of nerves.

JS: You've got a target for when you get stressed out, and it is a cathartic thing, involving using your fingers and hand and eyes for aiming and shooting. And to me that is similar to making a film: the French philosopher Paul Virilio said the machine gun and camera were invented at the same time...

JK: I remember talking to Raymond Durgnat about that, and we were talking about war films and things like that and he thought there was a special genre: the machine gun film. And we both had seen **The Hunchback of Rome**[13], a film to see if you can get the chance. It was an Italian neo-realist film, about a kid from the slums who starts out fighting the Germans, leading all the kids, getting machine guns, then going rotten of course; turning bad (laughs). There are great machine gun sequences in it, everyone blasting [demonstrates]. We are rather used to it now, but I seem to remember that it was a bit of a shocker at the time, all those teenagers blasting away. But shooting's the same, you are right.

JS: My favorite machine gun movie is **Django**[14]. Django drags a coffin everywhere, then when he opens it up its got the weapon in it.

JK: I'm just a mild-mannered English water-colourist really.

※

¹ They were eventually screened at the Dover Street ICA (Institute Of Contemporary Art), an event which – according to Keen – has been largely forgotten except for his own fond memories, and those of David Curtis from the Arts Council.

² The British based Channel Four Television is responsible for co-producing various visual media based experimental and art films, in addition to co-funding feature films.

³ Straight to video films circumnavigate the mainstream of Hollywood film, and in many ways, parallel the B movies and second features of past decades.

⁴ John Ford directed various films including: *Stagecoach* (1939), *They Were Expendable* (1945), *Fort Apache* (1948), *Rio Grande* (1950), *The Searchers* (1956), and *The Man Who Shot Liberty Valance* (1962), amongst others.

⁵ Jeff Keen regularly performs – or orchestrates performances – with his films, these performances have incorporated: speeches, minor scenes of both creation and destruction, and live musical accompaniment by noise and avant-jazz musicians.

⁶ This interview took place following a screening of a video of Jeff performing in one of the hollow seaside arches on Brighton seafront. The performance depicted Keen talking, a racket of white noise, and images from films projected over both artist and the wall behind him. The hollow arch would later become a night club. The performance video was broadcast on Channel Four in 1983, as part of the *Eleventh Hour Documentary* strand. Note that many of the films are accompanied by collector's booklets, mirroring the paraphernalia and accoutrements of Hollywood blockbusters.

⁷ Robert Breer made collage films such as *Form Phases I* (1953), *Image By Image I* (1954), *Recreation I* (1956/7) and *Blazes* (1961), among others.

⁸ B movie actor Chuck Norris has appeared in: *Force Of One* (Paul Aaron, 1979), *Lone Wolf McQuade* (Steve Carver, 1983), *Missing In Action* (Joseph Zito, 1984), asinine Reaganite Red Scare movie *Invasion U.S.A* (Joseph Zito 1985), and *Sidekicks* (Aaron Norris, 1993), and many others.

⁹ *True Lies* (1994) directed by James Cameron, starred Arnold Schwarzenegger as a spy who keeps his double live secret from his wife Jamie Lee Curtis. A willfully stupid re-working of James Bond.

¹⁰ Ealing Studios produced many British Cinema classics including *The Lavender Hill Mob* (Charles Crichton, 1951), *The Man In the White Suit* (A. Mackendrick, 1951) and many more.

11 Hammer were responsible for producing multiple classics of British cinema, justifiably known for their horror films, and especially their Dracula and Frankenstein cycles, starring Peter Cushing and Christopher Lee, the company were also responsible for the production of films ranging from science fiction such as **The Quatermass Xperiment** (Val Guest, 1955), through comedies like **Watch It Sailor!** (Wolf Rilla, 1961), through to literary adaptations such as **She** (Robert Day, 1965), and television spin-offs such as **Love Thy Neighbour** (John Robbins, 1973).

12 The English ensemble film comedies, famous for their 'veiled' sexual - and occasionally fecal - references (in part camp manners comedies which trace the development of sexual mores throughout the sixties) each of which bore the title Carry On... emerged with **Carry On Sargeant** (1958) and lasted until the mid-seventies, on the way creating such low-brow classics as **Carry On Cruising** (1962), **Carry On Cleo** (1965), **Carry On Camping** (1971), and many others.

13 An Italian/French co-production **The Hunchback Of Rome** aka **Gobbo, Il** was directed by Carlo Lizzani, 1960.

14 Directed by Sergio Corbucci, **Django** (1968) was an inspirational and violent western, starring Franco Nero in the title role.

An Introduction to the Films of Tyler Hubby

Born in Stanford Hospital, South of San Francisco, Tyler Hubby has spent much of his life in California. He began filmmaking in his early teens, directing numerous horror films inspired by the classic exploitation movies of the seventies, *It's Alive* (Larry Cohen, 1974) being a perennial favorite. His early movies include **The Creeping Puke** (1980) and it's "more developed" sequel **The Puke Creeps Again** (1981), both made when Hubby was an "awkward, dorky [twelve year old] kid." These films, which are currently in storage in his father's house, would be screened at high-school to audiences of screaming, shouting kids. Tyler soon recognized the beauty of these films was that their silence created an aural space in which the audience could talk, their voices creating a spontaneous soundtrack to the film. As a result of this he became interested in the way in which the audience related to the cinema, and the way in which the audience could be challenged with the ways of viewing film.

At the age of fourteen, Hubby directed **Bladder Problems** (1982), a one-and-a-half minute short in which a prosthetic bladder – designed to create the illusion of swelling flesh – expands to ludicrous size before exploding in a shower of gaudy fake blood. Hubby's next film was *Georgewalk* (1984) which took eighteen months to complete. The slow-paced, marijuana influenced, quasi-existential *Georgewalk* follows the appearance of a man on a hillside – in a bolt of lightning – and his subsequent journey into the nearby small town. *Georgewalk* was an exercise in putting a figure within a landscape, and the film is characterized by stylized photography, as Hubby attempts to render the familiar geography uncanny.

Georgewalk was followed by *Tea My Lovely* (1987) which was produced while Hubby was at community college and had access to editing equipment. Like its predecessor, *Tea My Lovely* was an existentially themed movie, this time focusing on the disintegration of Tyler's first serious relationship. While *Georgewalk* was not story boarded, and was scored with one piece of music, in contrast to this *Tea My Lovely* was rigorously planned, and had a soundtrack constructed by Elisabeth Bartfai, who had previously worked on numerous films in Hungary.

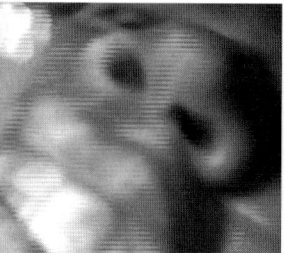 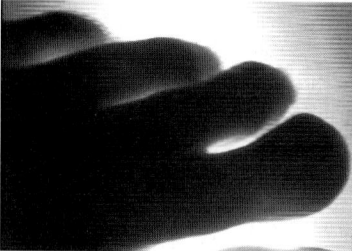 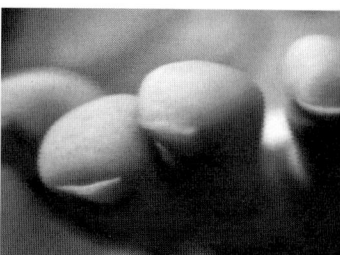

stills from **Webbed Feet**

Tyler Hubby's next film was **My Life With Webbed Feet** (1990). During a working trip to Los Angeles Hubby discovered his friend had webbed feet, and decided to use these as the central focus of his short film. **My Life With Webbed Feet** was shot immediately and edited in camera, with the sound dubbed on afterwards. Hubby: "We made the title slate at my friend's apartment on his Amiga Computer, took the tape out, put it in the camera, went over to my friend's house and shot the footage, then went back to the apartment and put the credits on. So it was all done – basically all the visuals were laid to tape in about two and a half hours".

Tyler Hubby graduated from the Art Institute Of San Francisco, where he studied with George Kuchar and Ernie Gehr. As Tyler remembers: "I had fun with George, I studied with Ernie Gehr, he's fairly well known for his minimal technically-oriented films, such as **Terminal Velocity**. It was kind of interesting having those two guys, because I felt that in some ways I was

stills from **Desktop**

stills from **Tea My Lovely**

doing work that fit in their parameters. Like the video work has a more lurid, melodramatic Kuchar quality, and the film piece that I did when I was doing Independent Study with Geer, which is way more formal, arranged". At college Hubby directed two pieces, **Desktop** (1993) and **Monday 9:02am** (1994). **Desktop** – produced by Hubby without the aid of any crew – was shot on video, and starts with the director's hand opening a drawer on a desk, removing a tape machine, and pressing 'play'. The tape consists of a woman's voice, asking Tyler to pick up the phone. As the tape progresses, the voice becomes increasingly angry, hysterically, and – finally – tearfully desperate, as she begs Tyler to answer. As the tape runs, so the camera tracks across the desktop, focusing on the accouterments of the commonplace which litter its surface. Finally the director's hand once again enters the frame, and switches off the tape player, returning it to the drawer. End.

Desktop was conceived and shot by Hubby over a two hour period

stills from **Desktop**

one evening, returning from a screening at the ATA, following his rediscovery of the answerphone tape. For Hubby the making of the film "was crossing a boundary, because of my relationship with her, maybe I was violating privacy, something like that". Hubby also acknowledges that **Desktop** has been accused of "exploiting [the] woman's emotional condition", however he also draws attention to the fact the film also places his own personal life on the screen. As a video **Desktop** functions on a series of plateaus; simultaneously an exercise in cold, clinical sadism, yet also, because of its emphasis on incongruous imagery with which to contrast the tearful tape, reminiscent of George Kuchar's work in which the everyday is invested with meaning via thunderously melodramatic scores. The film also creates an atmosphere in which the audience are held in a state of suspension, unable to fully identify either with the hand that turns on the tape, nor with the voice on the tape. As Hubby states, he "was really interested in the contrast between the detached neutrality in the surveying of objects on the desk, and the just completely heightened emotional state of the tape recording. And when I first showed this to some people I was going to show this at the Art Institute and they said, `Are you sure you want to show this? It's really self indicting, it really makes you look bad, just like a really hardened cynical bastard'. Because the camera, if that was representing me, is just so detached from the emotional state the voice is in".

Desktop was followed by **Monday 9:02am**. In contrast to its predecessor this was shot with a full crew, using a 400 foot/11 minute load of 16mm film, a camera with a 10mm lens, and two Nagra recorders. The

stills from **Monday 9:02am**

Montano Sokolow (seated) and Tyler Hubby on the set of **Monday 9:02am**
Photo by Bettina Herzner

film consists of a single stationary shot, overlooking a table in an apartment next to a window, and the street from the window. The film begins with a view of a man sweeping the street, the camera pulling-back through the window and into the apartment. Here, a man is preparing a cup of coffee at the table, smoking a cigarette and reading a book. The telephone rings, and he speaks, from the nature of the conversation the audience are lead to believe that he is talking with an old girlfriend. As the conversation progresses – becoming increasingly tense - the kettle whistles. As he pours his coffee the camera begins to track through the window and into the street, where a man collapses next to the street cleaner. The man in the apartment tells the woman on the phone what has happened, and leaving the receiver on the table runs down to investigate. The soundtrack combines his conversation with the street cleaner as he checks the convulsing stranger, and the woman's voice on the phone demanding he answer her. The man returns to the apartment to dial 911, meanwhile, through the window, the convulsing man stands and walks on. The sweeper resumes his work. The man in the apartment realizes what has happened and apologizes for dialing the emergency services. He sits down. The phone starts to ring again.

Monday 9:02am is shot in actual time, and contains no edits, it exists as a simple exploration of a moment of time in the lives of the characters. The film is simultaneously about nothing whatsoever, and also about a whole series of events, from the angry phone call, to the man collapsing in the street. Yet no single event is designed to give the film any sense of totalizing narrative, rather they all exist as independent yet interconnected aspects. As Hubby suggests, the film transforms the mundane elements of the everyday, and these become fascinating when viewed on the screen as the film demands its audience look at "nothing" in a different way. The film is a studied attempt to focus on small elements, which, Hubby notes, are "actual elements:" such as fire in form of the cigarette, and water in the coffee. For Tyler the film's carefully crafted minimalism opens up possibilities for a multiplicity of interpretations, allowing the audience to focus on any one of the many elements.

What *Monday 9:02am* and *Desktop* do share is the device of the

stills from **Drive To Work**

female voice on the phone, which in both cases is constructed as a source of confrontation, which erupts across the text. Tyler refuses to be drawn on the reason for such a device, simply stating that he does not "know why I keep going back to these forms". The instantaneous nature of video, already apparent in **Desktop**, and the emphasis on temporality envisioned in **Monday 9:02am**, became the central focus for Hubby's subsequent films, "I became obsessed with that process for those next three pieces. It was almost like the process became a big part of it. I didn't want to labour over it, I didn't want to have to deal with shooting footage and editing it. Also the thing with 8mm – you lose so much resolution the first generation down, that I wanted to keep everything first generation on the tape. So the whole idea was edit in camera. You know I'd go back and check my work as I am going, but the whole thing is a linear process, I can only go back and re-do the last shot. But I got really into doing that, capitalising on that creative burst. So you just feel like really doing something for the next three or four hours and not spending the next two or three weeks doing it up". In part this approach was a reaction again the laborious process of filmmaking; "I guess there was a whole thing where I was sick of the process. I want something immediate, like someone who is going out on stage and playing a song. Or free improvisation. Who knows where we'll end up? We may end up with something good, because we always do. Kind of like a leap of faith. It was really liberating being able to do that, because I've always been someone who is very intricate with story boards, and very into the process, and I was just feeling so bogged down in it. So I was just like this is a video camera, let's make it up as we go. Maybe its a short attention span, but also, as I said to capitalize on that original excitement and original creative burst. So it's like riding that one wave, rather than having to go back and try and catch the wave over and over again, just make that one count. And I got really into this idea of making a completely finished film in one day".

In 1992 Hubby produced **Valentine's Day**. Shot at a period when neither Tyler, nor his roommates, had girlfriends, the film was an exercise in the "celebration of solitude". With each member of the crew purchasing some of the props, the film was shot in one day, once again using in-camera editing. The film consists of a series of shots deconstructing and celebrating Valentine's Day; images of sweets with sugar-coated messages in love-hearts, flowers, and anatomical drawings make up the central images of the film, and the camera swoops from one image to the next, cutting back and forth, until the familiar images of celebration emerge as cynical and bitter fragmentations of love and desire. In the shooting of **Valentine's Day** – which was entirely improvised on the day – Hubby attempted to let his unconscious take over, and tried to create an undifferentiated flow of material, dictated by the excitement of the improvisation rather than any overriding grand schematic or conceptual gesture.

Hubby followed **Valentine's Day** with the video **Drive To Work**, shot in 1990 as a test piece using a newly acquired camcorder. Shot by Tyler as he drove to work on his birthday, **Drive To Work** consists entirely of a point of view shot from Tyler's perspective. Originally a test of endurance, the video emerged as a text in 1997 when Hubby framed it with specific credits at the

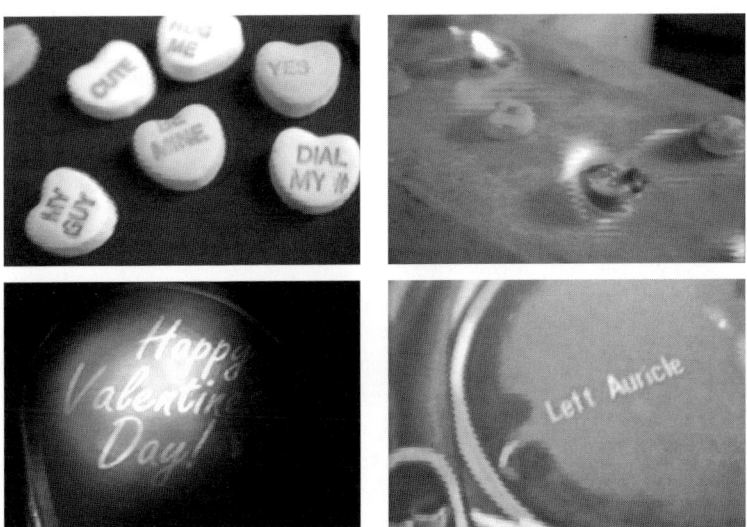

stills from **Valentine's Day**

opening which state the day and time at which he drove to work "with a hangover", the film ends as he enters his workplace and his colleagues offer birthday greetings. The piece was going to be called **Happy Birthday**, but the title was considered by Tyler to be too deceptive, and he eventually chose the more descriptive name which offered the viewer a sense of resolution. As Tyler states the film is "about getting there, I guess". In the plotless **Drive To Work** the most subtle event becomes a moment invested with meaning, for example, halfway through the film the camera's battery runs out and the piece hangs suspended whilst it is changed. **Drive To Work** is the peak of Hubby's minimalist films, and consolidates the temporal thematic introduced in **Monday 9:02am**, and **Valentine's Day**. All three of these films explore the notion of time within film, from the 11 minute slow-zooms of **Monday 9:02am**, through the unconscious flow of **Valentine's Day**, and into the literal experience of a journey.

In his explorations of cinematic temporality in **Drive To Work** and **Monday 9:02am** Hubby demands his audience experience a cinema of time, which transforms the commonplace into an aesthetic. In these films multiple, disparate elements coalesce to form meanings, for example the music on the car radio in **Drive To Work**, or the overflowing coffee cup in **Monday 9:02am**, neither of which has any recognized meaning, but both of which become momentary signifiers. Hubby's work demands that the audience re-imagine the everyday world around them, and perceive the everyday in a new way, this desire to re-engage with the mundane also becomes a central element in **Desktop**, in which the objects across the desk become the focus for the audience's gaze. Where **Drive To Work** differs from its predecessors is in its lack of preparation, whilst **Monday 9:02am** was a carefully constructed spacio-temporal exploration, **Drive To Work** is purely random and exists only as a film because Hubby chose to name it as such. The metanarrative around **Drive To Work**, therefore, also engages with the very question of video itself, asking at what point a recognizable text emerges from undifferentiated raw footage. In framing a specific flow of text Hubby has made a conscious decision to present the randomly chosen everyday event as a work in its own right.

Hubby's films raise questions about the nature of narrative and minimalism, from the rigorously orchestrated **Monday 9:02am** through to the spontaneous **Valentine's Day** and into the random **Drive To Work**. All of these films reveal temporal concerns and each focuses on the relationship between glimpsing at a moment in time, yet they all suggest widely differing interpretations of Hubby's temporal project.

Dephtography and Non-Linear Animation:

The World of M. Henry Jones.

M. Henry Jones is a New York based animator, who as a child was inspired by various types and styles of animation, ranging from "the man" Chuck Jones' *One Froggy Evening*[1], and – later – to underground filmmaker Harry Smith's epic *Heaven and Earth Magic*[2]. M. Henry Jones began directing and producing a string of animation shorts, producing his first, *The 3 Fertknuckles* at the age of twelve. As he states:
"I always liked animation because it was always something that was different, it was very secret... because, if you're a kid between 3 and 10, everything is impressive: it blows your mind. Then, when you get to 10 years old, you start to learn there are somethings you can do yourself, but it is very hard to do animation yourself, so I always kind of hung around, like, an unsolved problem..."
Now an acclaimed animator Jones encourages children to animate, and, on occasion, has been known to give a would-be animator complete sets of animation pencils, paper and guide books.
In 1979 Jones produced *Go Go Girl*, a flick-book as film, featuring animated photographs of a woman dancing the 'pony' against a background of optically printed vertical lines, the resulting film was the first of a trilogy of music films. The second, *Soul City* (1979) again used a combination of animation and live action in order to create a unique visionary style, and the film later became a large influence on the rock promo-video. The third in this series of music movies was the rockabilly influenced *Brand New Cadillac*.
In October 1986 M. Henry Jones was invited by Tessa Hughes-Freeland and Ela Troyano to screen his work at the 3rd Annual New York Downtown Film Festival[3], alongside a screening of his films, Jones also presented a 3D side show. At the festival, Jones met R. Anthony Munn, who shared his interest in 3D – as Jones states: "between us we have every fucking stereo camera ever made". Alongside Munn, Jones began to increase his experimentation with various kinds of 3D photography, much of which was – like alchemy – a forgotten science which has been artistically neglected, prematurely discarded, relegated to the dustbin of historical novelty, where it was, at best, viewed as a kitsch joke.
The resulting experiments in 3D photography and animation

enabled Jones to begin directing and co-producing Dephtographical pictures: 3D pictures, which are made up from a multiplicity of marginally different images, that become animated as the viewer walks around them. The images Jones utilises for his Dephtographical pictures vary greatly; some are classic American pop icons, such as 'The Lone Ranger', whose horse rises up on its back legs as the viewer's position changes, or a boxing match in which a punch is thrown, while in the background the audience can be seen jumping and throwing their hats in the air, other images appear to have come from Fifties advertising; such as a car which races through the depths of deep space toward the viewer. Besides these manifestations of classic Americana, Jones has also produced a Dephtographic picture based on artist James Romberger's *Thirst*, a comic book adaptation of the youthful street hustling experiences of artist, writer, filmmaker, and political activist David Wojnarowicz[4]. Other pictures are abstract, depicting patterns of chequered squares, which transmutate before the viewer into a spiralling cyclic image. Jones is also developing a dephtography badge, which – over 9 images – depicts the transmutation of a pig into a duck.

Besides working with Dephtography, Jones currently works producing animated advertisements for television, and describes the experience as analogous to "making a hot-rod car, it's like going up against the Miller Car at the N.H.R.A – National Hot Rod Association. That is the same shit to me. I'm trying to make a commercial that can be as strong against the other stuff on the TV. They have all types of power; they have computers, they have all [that] shit, they have everything. And we are over there trying to make a commercial that can sell as many eye-glasses as the next guy, and my whole TV commercial shit was always about the Fifties, every time we had a situation I would always say; 'Well, lets see if we can solve this like the Fifties'. And that was a good scam, that worked out okay. Because I don't really want to get involved in trying to solve animation like they do now. They solve that thing in so many ways you can't even figure it out. I'm just a guy over here trying to make art. I make a TV commercial, I try to make a really arty one..." M. Henry Jones is also currently working with director Rachel Amodeo[5] and writer, actress, musician, and artist Dame

Darcy[6] on the short film, provisionally titled **Rest In Peace**.

On Dephtography

Jack Sargeant: I want to start by asking you how you initially became interested in the Dephtography animation?

M. Henry Jones: [I was] always interested in that, I had a teacher at the School Of Visual Art, his name was Lowel Bodger, he said to me, 'You know, film is interesting, but it always runs at the same speed, and I like this winky stuff – the stuff that blinks – because it has a non-linear time image.' So, you know, I made some phone calls, I tried to find out how to make it, I got hold of this guy at a place called Ciniview, Ciniview was in the Bronx. And nobody ever wanted to help you, because it was animation, but all they wanted was like a client with enough money to buy a plastic peanut and sell to some idiot in a cereal box. So the problem was keeping them on the phone, they're like 'Do you have half a million dollars?' I'm like 'No, but can we talk?' 'No, we're not talking to you, we're talking to people who have half a million dollars. Get off the phone!'

JS: How did you do it then, did you just experiment and figure it out for yourself?

MHJ: R. Anthony Munn [Bob] – he's going to invite everybody to see my Slatterpus picture tonight. Him and me, we just figured it out. Bob figured it out. Because the lenticular animation is so complex that I never really wanted to go there, but Bob did – so Bob went there. So now Bob can make a picture with a lenticular screen. I can't. I can't go into a darkroom right now and make that picture, it's too hard. But Bob can, and he does everyday of his life. And he is my partner – you know – we have a company it is R. Anthony Munn, Arvy, Gary Darrow, Sara – Bob's girlfriend – Sara Cook, she is a person who knows a lot about 3D, all those people from Dephtography.
There is no Dephtography without R. Anthony Munn. I am an

animator, I'm not a photo technology wizard like this guy.

I struggle with the art, I can't draw, I can't sculpt: I'm a director, I can't really make 'art'. Yeah, I know how to make art: you get some fucking goddamn canvas that's bigger than a fucking billboard then you get some oil painting and sell it for $1,000,000 – I can't paint that shit. Man, I don't know nothing about it. I'm a director, I take people that, you know, want to be that person and want to work in animation, they have talent, and I help them with me to get to the finish line with out getting killed. But I don't have to have any talent in that area, because it's not my game. My game is to get to the finish line with the shit. Like Bob Munn, here's Bob Munn, he's gonna help me get to the finishing line with my shit tonight. But, you know, my assistant [on Slatterpus], she doesn't know a goddamn thing about animation, except she's not dumb enough to not listen to me, so she listens to me and we get to the finishing line, and we get this shit to Bob. Bob makes it, 'cos Bob knows how to make it in the darkroom, and then, if everything goes haywire, he gives it to Sara and they scan it into the computer domain and fix all the stupid shit I could not do, until it is right.

JS: *What do you see as the difference between the film animation you used to do and the Dephtography?*

MHJ: Dephtography has a non-linear time dimension, that's the difference. There's no more Maltese Falcon you know, you know the Maltese Cross? You know about the Maltese Cross?

JS: *What's that?*

MHJ: The thing that spins on the projector that makes it go at speed[7]. That shit is over. I don't want to make animated films, they have a singular time dimension – I wanted a non-linear time dimension.

JS: *What do you see as important about the non-linear time dimension?*

MHJ: It makes the... it turns the artwork into an interactive moment. I could spend the rest of my life making a film that was like ten seconds long, and they'd have to run it over and over and over again, except that now with the non-linear time dimension we can just have people stand in front of it....

JS: And look as long as they want.

MHJ: Look as long as they want, go ahead! Get involved! My favorite part is frame minus 12 against frame minus 11. Film, before you even turn it on, the shit's over. With dephtography it's not, you can sit there and say "wow", "look at this", "look at this", "oh yeah". That's happening, you can't do that with film. Movies are bullshit.

Slatterpus

MHJ: Slatterpus is my one idea – you know how like I was bitchin' about how I have no talent for art? Well I did one time have a dream, and in that dream I saw this guy and he was telling me something – and I was standing on this water wheel that was turning... going away from him... [Jones' story is interrupted by a phone call from Rachel Amodeo, Jones tells her that he is unable to talk because; "I'm meeting this man, I'm being interviewed on National TV right now!"]...

JS: You were talking about Slatterpus?

MHJ: I was running on this waterwheel and, like, this Slatterpus was trying to tell me something, and I couldn't... I was trying to stand up on this wheel and listen to him, and he was saying all these really important things, but I was so wasted in my dream I couldn't even remember what it was, but I did fucking-mother-fucking remember this guy, like, yelling at me or something. That's where Slatterpus came from.

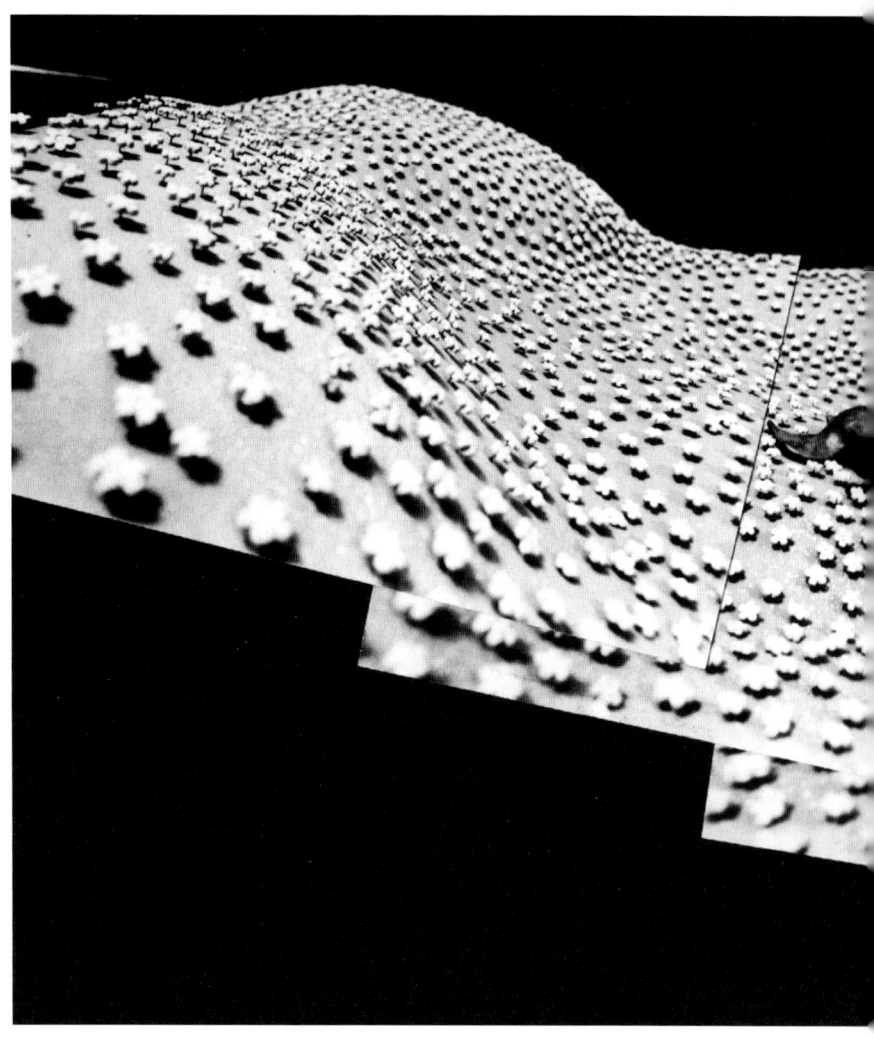

Cinema Contra Cinema

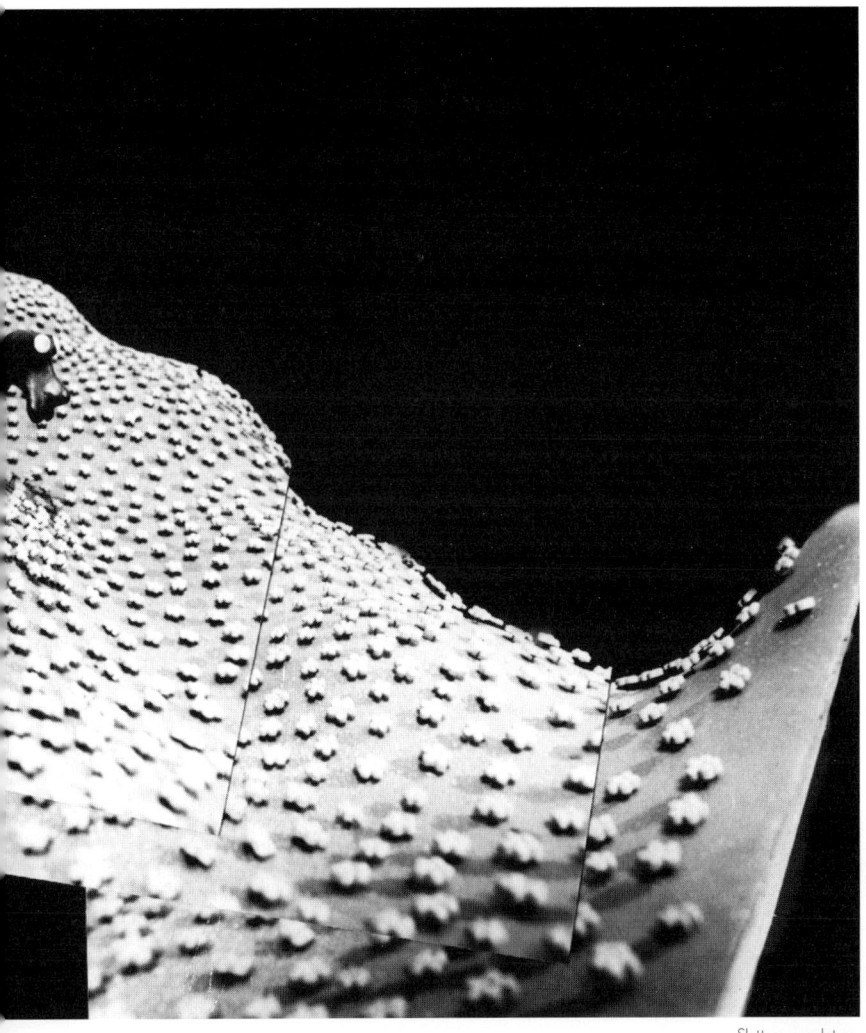

Slatterpus sculpture

JS: *That inspired the picture?! Who did the sculpture of Slatterpus?*

MHJ: An assistant did the clouds, I made Slatterpus, and Gary Daryl also, he helped a lot.

Vari-Vue Vs Dephtography

MHJ: He [Munn] was crying about this picture of a woman holding a shoe – the woman with the shoe – and I said 'that's gotta be a Vari-Vue", and he's like 'I don't think so', and I'm like 'Hey man, I've never seen a 3D picture that you could not turn over on the back and see the word Vari-Vue". And he said, 'It doesn't say that man. It's not on it. It's something else'. I'm going, 'Wow that's wild. But I bet you a million dollars to a penny that that's a Vari-Vue'. But it wasn't. It was a picture by W.N Draper, in 1932, its really early fucking 3D artwork. And me and him went over to this guy's place and I brought it from the guy for $125, and Bob was like shock-rocked. He was like,'What you just brought that? I would have paid $1000 for that. I've got $1000 in my pocket. Why did he sell it to you?'. I said,'Hey look – do I know? I own it, we'll look at it together'. So then he came over to my house and we looked at the photo and we tried to understand how it was made, but... Then he calls me about a week, nine days, later, 'You want to go to the Vari-Vue auction?' I'm like 'Yeah, lets go'. So we go to the Vari-Vue auction and end up getting this other guy to spend all his money to buy all this shit, and I was going to make it into jewelry and all that didn't work out...

JS: *So what is Vari-Vue?*

MHJ: Vari-Vue — that's another thing – we are not trying to push Vari- Vue, we are not trying to promote Vari-Vue. We are trying to promote Dephtography! But Vari-Vue was a similar thing to what we do, but Vari-Vue never quite took it to our limits. We crush the limits on lenticular photography, we're limit crushers!

This interview transpired in M. Henry Jones workshop on New York's Avenue A prior to the unveiling of the picture: Slatterpus at Max Fisches (aka Max Fish), a bar on the Lower East Side. Due to his insanely hectic schedule M. Henry Jones had been awake for two days at the time of this interview, in order that he could complete the modelling of miniature plastic fifties-style televisions, which form the frame to dephtographical images of The Lone Ranger which would be sold at the evening's opening. Throughout the interview Jones would periodically pause in order to check the modelling of the plastic televisions. M. Henry Jones is also exceptionally supportive of other New York artists, and the interview was paused firstly so that he could discuss the benefits of 16mm film with writer/musician/punk originator Richard Hell, and later in order that he could introduce me to Peter, one of the founders of the notorious underground newspaper the East Village Other, and show me a photograph of Yippie Jerry Rubin.

[1] Chuck Jones worked as an animator and director for Warner Brothers, where he worked on many of the company's most famous short-animated films, including ***Injun Trouble*** (1938), ***Baby Buggy Bunny*** (1954), ***Ali Baba Bunny*** (1957), and ***One Froggy Evening*** (1955). ***One Froggy Evening*** – produced as a part of the 'Merrie Melodies' series – focused on a workman who finds a singing frog. Unfortunately, the frog will sing only for the workman, and he is thus unable to capitalize on this wonder. Not only did Jones direct the film, he also collaborated with Milt Franklyn and Michael Maltese on the song 'Michigan Rag' which was used in the soundtrack of the film. "Animation," said Jones, "isn't the illusion of life... it is life!"

[2] Harry Smith was a filmmaker, magician, anthropologist, musicologist, and visionary. His numerically titled hand-painted films, animations, and superimpositions create a cinema of hypnogogic wonder (see Jack Sargeant, *Naked Lens: Beat Cinema*, Creation Books, 1997).

[3] The New York Downtown Film Festival existed as a forum for a wide variety of underground filmmakers, it ran from 1984 - 1986 (see Jack Sargeant, *Deathtripping: The Cinema of Transgression*, 1995).

4 David Wojnarowicz was a visual artist, writer, filmmaker, and activist. His early life was exceptionally brutal, and he ended up living on the street. As an artist his work dealt with numerous topics, including homophobia, desire, freedom, sexuality, rebellion and autobiographical material. (see Jeri Cain Rossi, 'David Wojarowicz (1954 - 1992)' in Jack Sargeant, *Deathtripping: The Cinema of Transgression*, Creation Books, 1995, and David Wojnarowicz *Close To The Knives: A Memoir of Disintergration*, Serpents Tail, 1991/1992)

[5] Rachel Amadeo wrote, produced, directed, and stared in the feature film ***What About Me?***, a vivid portrait of a homeless woman living in New York. M. Henry Jones assisted in the camera work on the film.

[6] Dame Darcy is the artist responsible for, amongst other things, the surrealistic Victorian influenced comic *Meat Cake*, published by Fantagraphics (see Jack Sargeant, *Suture*, Creation Books, 1998).

7 The Maltese Cross is a part of the intermittent movement of the projector, this works by pulling the film at a speed, dictated by the film's perforations. It is this movement which creates cinema.

No Beer, Some Movies, And A Lot of Rain.

The 4th Chicago Underground Film Festival Diary

This diary is cobbled together from notes written on a plane to San Francisco from Chicago, and on a plane from San Francisco to New York. There were a lot more filmmakers, and a lot more good films, than those I necessarily saw. Other highlights of the festival (mostly stuff which I'd either seen before, or was reliably informed was good) included: *Premenstrual Spotting* by Machiko Saito, *The Rainbow Man* by Sam Green, *Fame Whore* by Jon Moritsugu, *(The Elaborate) Empire Of Ache* by Lisa Hammer, *Rock And Roll Punk, The Trailer* by Jim Sikora, *Splatter Film* by Mike Kuchar, *Pump With A Chump* by Modi & Adam Cohen, *Law of Desire: Clit-O-Matic: Part Two Of The Adventures of White Trash Girl* by Jennifer Reeder, *Drive To Work* by Tyler Hubby, *Sore Losers* by John Michael McCarthy, *The Second Cumming* by Mike Diana, and *The Bride Of Frank* by Steve Ballot, amongst others.

Special thanks to Mark and Fran who regularly let me sleep at their apartment, to everybody at Chicago Underground Film Festival who were kind enough to invite me, and to Charles & Marne for their support and assistance in the preparation of this diary.

Monday 11th August.
    I'm going to Chicago to launch my new book *Naked Lens: Beat Cinema*, unfortunately UPS are on strike. My books are possibly stuck with the distributors in San Francisco, I will have to carry some over with me. They weigh a lot. Shit. To further complicate matters I bashed my foot a few nights back, and the toe has turned a glorious purple red. It hurts to walk on it and I decide to go to the doctor. Unfortunately he declares it septic and prescribes penicillin. He then tells me that I can not drink for one week. This pisses me off as I am leaving for Chicago on Wednesday, a trip which necessitates two flights just to get there, at least one of which serves free booze. It also means that I can't luxuriate in discount beers at the festival.

Tuesday 12th August.
    Get travellers cheques. Pack bags. Check insurance. Pay bills. Leave details with people. Reconfirm flights.

Donna Jagela, CUFF festival director with Jack Sargeant
Photo © Marne Lucas, 1997

Wednesday 13th August.
    Thanks to the wonders of temporality I arrive in Chicago only four hours after I left, despite a ten hour journey via Boston, I feel totally exhausted. Take a taxi straight to the Theater Building on West Belmont. The festival has just started - the opening night feature being Frank Grow's **Love God**. I dump my bag in a small office which is full to overflowing with rucksacks/suitcases etc. Jay Bliznick (Festival Director) and Donna Jagela (Program Editor) entertain me with stories, introduce me to people, and pour coffee down my throat, in the Theater lobby/ bar. As the film finishes the audience emerge singing its praises. I hook up with Brian Wendorf (Programming Director), Wendy Solomon (Administrative Assistant) – both of whom were my hosts when I was in town last year to do a *Deathtripping* show – and Mark **Affliction** Hejnar who introduces me to Marne Lucas, who collaborated with Jacob Pander on the award winning infrared erotic short **The Operation**, and Charles Pinion, director of pulp video classics **Red Spirit Lake** and **We Await**. At some point

we head over to a party. A local band tries to entertain the throng of jet lagged filmmakers with their renditions of cheesy film themes, the two girls they have dancing with them are pretty cute, especially during the Goldfinger theme. Mark and I leave at around 2:00am. We end up talking until 4:00am-ish in his kitchen.

Thursday 14th August.
Jet lag/daylight/the suddenly friendly cat conspire to awaken me at 8:00am. I stare at the ceiling for an hour trying to get back to sleep but eventually give up. Mark is up soon after. His new short *Bible Of Skin* is premiering this evening. We spend the day hanging out. I confirm my book signing at Quimby's, a really good shop which specializes in underground comics, fanzines, small press, etc, and is decorated with original artworks by various counter culture celebrities. We head over to the Theater in the early evening.

The festival is programmed in two screens in the Theater Building, the first is for film, the second for video projection. This means that movies are playing against each other, but the enthusiasm of the locals and the hoards of filmmakers means that both cinemas have at least 75% capacity continually (and often 100%). Before Mark's screening I am introduced to Sarah Jacobson, the woman behind *I Was A Teenage Serial Killer* and – last year's opening feature – *Mary Jane's Not A Virgin Anymore*.

Bible Of Skin is playing in a screening which includes *The Erotic Adventures Of Alex The Clown* by teenage animator Keith Schofield. The film appears to have no moral values whatsoever, as the main character goes to the city in order to get laid, eventually choosing a crack whore for the purpose. Naturally the audience lap up the film's bad taste.

Jennifer Cluck's *Five Hits* is next, a short movie depicting a 14-year old-girl after taking five doses of acid. The girl bleats and screams as the image swirls and twists in a series of psychedelic gyres.

Bible Of Skin is a combination of stock/found/original/home movie footage, which has been run through an aesthetic and optical blender by Hejnar, to a create new images which have been distorted and manipulated to make a film with an almost lyrical structure. Each segment of the video is distinct from its predecessor, yet builds up on the thematic of obsession, religion, ritual, warfare, sex, and family. The film goes down well, especially the castration sequence.

Following Mark's movie is Cindy Kleine's scatological essay **Holy Matter**. The artist and various friends obsess on the topics of fecal matter and bowel movements, in a short film which is frequently punctuated by home-movie footage of the director-as-little-girl playing with the toilet and watching as her shit is flushed away. Bizarre.

Finally George Kuchar's **Vermin Of The Vortex** is screened. This film begins with diary footage of George at last years CUFF (where he was the guest of honour), before being abducted by aliens and forced to lecture at some bourgeoisie college. The entire film has a great score, no doubt culled from George's now legendary record archives.

Blinking from the screening we emerge and flee for drinks (non alcoholic yet again for me), before returning to the Theater to watch Charles Gatewood's **True Blood**, a ritual blood letting short, and Charles Pinion's **I Get Ideas** a juxtapostionary collage short. These are followed by the hour long documentary **Straight To You, Nick Cave: A Portrait**, directed by Nanni Jacobson. Much as I like Nick Cave, my eyes won't stay open so I head off to the evening's sponsored bar. Here we meet cinematic ubermensch – and director of such classics as **My Sweet Satan**, **Deadbeat At Dawn**, and **Roadkill** – Jim Van Bebber who has come in to showcase his legendary, and now nearly completed, feature epic **Charlie's Family**, which is scheduled for the following evening. The film isn't an official entry into the festival, but a late night preview – and the American premier.

Friday 15th August.
    Still only got four hours sleep.
    Today we had to get up early for the filmmaker's breakfast. CUFF are buying everybody bagels and coffee. Over breakfast we get to meet Todd Morris and Deborah Twiss who have directed and produced **A Gun For Jennifer**, which is playing tomorrow. Dame Darcy (the visionary artist behind

Booksigning at Quimby's Queer Store, Chicago
Shade Rupe, Dame Darcy and Jack Sargeant
Photo © Marne Lucas, 1997

Jack Sargeant and Wendy Solomon at Uncle Fun, Chicago
Photo © Marne Lucas, 1997

Meat Cake comic, and star of Lisa Hammer's *(The Elaborate) Empire Of Ache* and numerous other projects too diverse to go into here) has also turned up, as has Eric Brummer, and Jeff Krulick. Sarah Jacobson and Marne Lucas ask me what sex scenes in films turn me on, I can't think of very many, and admit I don't often get aroused by movies. At about midday a contingent leave the Theater building and head up the street to the greatest shop in Chicago: Uncle Fun. Every time I am in town I visit this emporium of trash, as – apparently – does everybody else. The entire store is given over to tin toys, odd T-shirts, badges from long forgotten elections, Jesus tea towels, luminous religious oddities, promotional tie-ins from various neglected movies, plastic jewelry, etc.

Writer and filmmaker Jerry Tartaglia is in town with the recently restored prints of Jack Smith's movies - including the believed-to-have-been-lost *No President* (1968 - 1997), *Flaming Creatures* (1961), and *Normal Love* (1963) – I make a point of going to watch No President, which depicts a bizarre tableau juxtaposing various of Smith's 'creatures' against footage of presidential candidate Wendle Winkie. All scored with Martin Denny tunes culled from Smith's collection of musical exotica. Anarchism has never looked so good. Afterwards I pester Jerry to discuss his restoration and dissemination of Smith's work with me, although this conversation is cut short due to the start of the Jeff Krulick retrospective.

Charles and I get great seats and laugh like fools at Krulick's twisted world view. The retrospective includes the awesome (and much bootlegged) *Heavy Metal Parking Lot* in which Krulick and collaborator John Heyn film the audience at a Judas Priest arena show while they wait for the doors to open.

The film's depiction of drunk teens, hot groupies, and stoner metalheads is both visionary and witty, but avoids descending into satire, primarily because Krulick has the wisdom to know when to edit. Sure, the film laughs at the metal audience, but with more affection than contempt. The sequel is also shown entitled **Neil Diamond Parking Lot**, it depicts the same arena parking lot, which this time is swamped by middle aged couples, who — unbelievably — are remarkably similar to the metal kids of the previous movie. Krulick also screened several other films, including the incredible **Ernest Borgnine On Tour**, in which the actor and his son — pursued by Krulick — drive across America on their summer vacation in their massive $700,000 coach. Like most of Krulick's films this is notable for its severely skewed view of American life.

Following this screening we don't even leave the cinema because next up is Eric Brummer's **Electric Flesh**. This is basically a stop-motion animation explosion of flaming skulls/ eye balls/ exploding bodies etc. Kind of like the last ten minutes of the **Evil Dead**. Great. This is followed by **Baked Alaska**, a documentary by Huck Botko about the 'joys' of family 'reunions'. Huck goes to visit his mother, who left the family when he was a kid, and — in honour of the last meal he had with her — Botko makes mom a baked alaska. Only he adds some choice ingredients, primarily scrapings from maggot riddled roadkill. One of the best/most disturbing films I've seen in a long time. Huck's hatred of his family is visionary. Although there was more on the program I was getting hungry (seriously) and Charles, Wendy, Marne, and I split for pizza (vegetarian), returning at midnight for Mike White's excellent kick-in-the-ass to Hollywood new boy Tarantino **You're Not Fooling Anybody**, which juxtaposes Tarantino's non-original text with the... uh... previously produced, original Hong Kong feature **City On Fire**. This was followed by **You're Still Not Fooling Anybody** which further annihilates the myth of QT as auteur, by revealing the 'links' between **Pulp Fiction** and various other features. White's movies were followed by the long awaited, much talked about, Jim Van Bebber premier.

Even before the film (screened as a 'rough' edit on video) started ,there was an atmosphere of palpable tension, excitement was in the air. Jim stood up to introduce the movie and was promptly blinded by the flashing lights of a dozen cameras. When the applause died down Jim basically said, "Oh, I've been making this movie for nine years. Hope you like it. It just needs a few edits, and wipes and fade outs till it's done".

Charlie's Family blew the audience away.

It was that good.

Somewhat unnervingly – given my previous day's talk with Sarah and Marne about sex in films – I have to admit that I found one of the actresses playing a Manson family girl in the movie to be pretty hot, especially when she stops having sex with some guy in order to describe Helter Skelter in detail, crouching naked in the pissing rain. When I relate the anecdote to Jim he shakes my hand, declaring me a fellow sick puppy.

Saturday 16th August.

Still very little sleep, up early to do press on my new book *Naked Lens*. The guy who is meant to interview me by phone from Los Angeles has vanished, or is not picking up the phone. This pisses me off for the morning.

I am then interviewed by Mark for a forthcoming documentary film project. At around 1:00pm Mark and I head for the cinema. My *Naked Lens* book launch starts at 2:00pm. I feel very fucking nervous. I know what I want to say, but I have nothing formally prepared. Luckily the talk goes well, and I detail production histories and anecdotes with ease. I don't realize until somebody glares at me that I've been talking for about 45 minutes. I wind things down and start the first of the two movies I've brought with me: Alfred Leslie & Robert Frank's **Pull My Daisy**, and Peter Whitehead's **Wholly Communion**. As far as anybody knows this is probably the American premier of Peter's movie (which I will screen in San Francisco the following weekend). While the film's play I wait outside, Beth B (one of the special guests) arrives for her screening – **Two Small Bodies** – which is also on this afternoon (her new video **Visiting Desire** is the closing night feature). Its good to see Beth, but we only have time for a brief chat.

After the film show and lengthy Q&A I'm driven downtown by Donna to Quimbys where I'm doing a signing with Dame Darcy and Shade

Jack Sargeant at CUFF, Chicago
Photo © Marne Lucas, 1997

Rupe (editor of *Funeral Party*). The signing is okay – Jerry Tartaglia, Charles and Marne all turn up, which is good of them – and Quimbys agree to buy all my remaining books, meaning I've – at last – got some money. While signing it begins to rain. And rain. And rain. Four hours later and there are no taxis, no buses and the street is flooded. Lightning burns up the otherwise black sky. Charles and Marne have to get back to the Theater to see Charles' movie *Madball*, he's just spent a couple of hundred dollars on 'getting a 16mm print made and there is NO TRANSPORT ANYWHERE. It is still raining and the Theater is twenty odd blocks away. Somehow someone offers a lift and Charles, Marne, and Shade vanish. A group of Meat Cake fans take Darcy away, and I'm left in Quimbys watching the rain. I try calling a cab but all companies are either busy/engaged/or the phone lines are down. This is grim as I envisage walking all that way in the rain. I call the Theater on Belmont, but Bryan is watching a film, and Jay has vanished. Whoever answers the phone doesn't appear to know who Wendy and Donna are.

Shit.

Just when I'm giving up all hope a car pulls up, it is Jay and Jim Van Bebber. I dive in the back and we shoot off. Jim is waving around a nearly empty bottle of whiskey. The two of them are arguing about the value of film schools (for the record Jim is in favour, while Jay is not). The road ahead is flooded, and - despite my urging that Jay just put his pedal to the metal and just aqua-glide - he pussies out (although – in fairness – it should be noted that Jay thinks that I'm a pussy for not walking back to the cinema). We end up driving around the whole of Chicago in the rain. Jay becomes increasingly worried because the water level is rising and it is his girlfriend's car and she wanted it back within twenty minutes. Jim and I tease him about this all the way back to Belmont. As we walk into the cinema Jay's girlfriend is by the door, Jay immediately apologizes (although she clearly isn't angry - he just has a guilty conscience), I try to cause more trouble for Jay, by thanking him for taking me and Jim to the local strip joint.

Meet Charles and Marne in the lobby, in the traffic chaos and floods they got lost on the way back to the cinema and missed Charles' movie, however Charles' brother Bill and his wife Linda have turned up and were able to see the movie. The five of us head for a Thai meal, and Beth B and Jay soon arrive too. Have time to talk to Beth, and thank Jay for everything.

After dinner (which Bill and Linda pay for, obviously familiar with Charles' poverty struck friends) we rush back to see **A Gun For Jennifer**, a 35mm feature by Todd Morris, written, produced by and starring Deborah Twiss. The film follows run-away housewife Allison as she flees to New York, gets attacked by some scum bags, and rescued by an all-woman vigilante group. Under pressure Allison is forced to join the group, and telling them her name is Jennifer, is soon out blasting various sleazeballs and rapists. Then the police and organized crime bosses become involved... **A Gun For Jennifer** is well paced, and tightly scripted, and everybody assembled for the screening loves it. Whether the film could truly said to be 'underground' is a different matter, as it is almost certainly going to be a break through for Morris and Twiss into the 'big time' of 'independent film'.

After the film I say good-bye to everybody, although I will see Charles and Sarah in San Francisco next week.

Back to Mark's house, and it's still raining. We sit and talk till 4:30am. I have to set my alarm for 7:00am, as I am flying to San Francisco in the morning to do a spoken word gig that evening, and the *Naked Lens* film show the following weekend at the ATA (Artists Television Access, a great space). This, unfortunately, means that I miss the Guest of Honour appearance by John Waters on Sunday (when I meet up with Charles Pinion and Sarah Jacobson in San Francisco later in the week they both tell me that John Waters was great. Marne later confirms this on the phone when I return to England ten days later.)

Sunday 17th August
    Sitting in the airport at 9:30am, waiting for my flight – which, thanks to the weather, has been delayed by a half hour – I wish I'd seen more movies, and drank some beer. I already miss hanging out with everybody and discussing movies. But, sitting watching the rain splash on the runway, I vow to return next year.

Appendix

Chewing Bubblegum and Underground Cinema first appeared in *Cups*, no.85, November 1997, and *Entropy*, no.3, volume 1, Fall 1997.

Aural Celluloid: Ten Brief Notes and Observations on Underground Film and Music first appeared in *World Art* no.19, winter 1998.

Tracing The Edge of Power: A Brief Introduction to the Film And Art of Beth B first appeared in *Art & Design/Art & Film*, no.49, 1996.

Screening Transgressive Desires: Crash Vs Hustler White first appeared in *Headpress* no.13, Autumn 1996.

Louder, Faster, Shorter: The Manny and Modi Shorts first appeared in *Fringecore* no.5, June/July 1998.

Human Wave: The Videos of Raymond Pettibon first appeared in *Fringecore* no.4, April/May 1998.

Plastic Porn Visionary: The Films of Eric Brummer first appeared in *Fringecore* no.6, August/September, 1998.

Swallow. The Bad Taste of Sweet Vengeance of Huck Botko, first appeared in *Headpress* no.18, Spring, 1999.

Documenting The Underground first appeared in *Headpress* no.14, Spring 1997.

True Stories About True Gore: The World of Monte Cazzaza first appeared in *Erupto! Official Organ of 1998 Volcano No-Budget Film Festival*, and formed the basis of a lecture that accompanied the screening.

Baby Blatzo Vs Dr Gaz: The Cinematic Visions of Mr Soft Eliminator Jeff Keen first appeared in *Kino Kaze*, no.4, no date.

An Introduction to the Films of Tyler Hubby first appeared in *Fringecore* no.8, January/February 1999.

Dephtography And Non-Linear Animation: The World of M Henry Jones first appeared in *Art & Design/Art & Animation*, no.53, 1997.

No Beer, Some Movies, And A Lot of Rain first appeared in *Headpress* no.16, Spring 1998.

Bibliography

Bataille, Georges, *The Tears Of Eros*, City Lights Books: San Francisco, 1989.

Dwoskin, Stephen, *Film Is...The International Free Cinema*, Overlook Press: Woodstock, 1975.

Hunter, Jack, *Inside Teradome: An Illustrated History Of Freak Film*, Creation Books: London, 1995.

Hunter, Jack, *Eros In Hell: Sex, Blood And Madness In Japanese Cinema*, Creation Books: London, 1998.

Kerekes, David, *Sex, Murder, Art: The Films Of Jorg Buttgereit*, Critical Vision: Stockport, 1994/1998.

Kerekes, David & Slater, David, *Killing For Culture: An Illustrated History Of Death Film, From Mondo To Snuff*, Creation Books: London, 1994.

Puchalski, Steven, *Slimetime: A Guide To Sleazy, Mindless, Movie Entertainment*, Critical Vision: Stockport, 1996.

Renan, Sheldon, *The Underground Film: An Introduction to Its Development In America*, Studio Vista: London, 1967/1971.

Rupe, Shade, ed, *Funeral Party*, Volume 2, Rude Shape: New York, 1997.

Sargeant, Jack, *Deathtripping: The Cinema Of Transgression*, Creation Books: London, 1995.

Sargeant, Jack, *Naked Lens: Beat Cinema*, Creation Books: London, 1997.

Sargeant, Jack, Suture: *The Arts Journal*, Volume 1, Creation Books: London, 1998.

Stevenson, Jack, *Desperate Visions 1: Camp America; John Waters, George & Mike Kuchar*, Creation Books: London, 1996.

Vogel, Amos, *Film As Subversive Art*, Weindenfold & Nicolson: London, 1974.

Weldon, Michael, with Beesley, Charles; Martin, Bob, and Fitton, Akira, *The Psychotronic Encyclopedia Of Film*, Plexus: London, 1989/1983.

Jack Sargeant is a hyperactive polymath. He is the author of the highly acclaimed critical explorations of underground and outlaw culture: *Deathtripping: The Cinema Of Transgression* (Creation Books, 1995), *Naked Lens: Beat Cinema* (Creation Books, 1997), and is editor of *Suture: The Arts Journal* (Creation Books, 1998). Sargeant's written work has appeared in numerous publications, including: *Headpress, Cups, Entropy, Fringecore, World Art, Art & Design*, and *Bizarre*, amongst others. He lectures widely on underground culture, and has curated numerous festivals and special events.

He is currently working on numerous book and film projects.

He lives in Brighton, England.